Carrying Hope

Expecting Death, Delivering Life

Beth Appleby

instant
apostle

First published in Great Britain in 2025

Instant Apostle
104A The Drive
Rickmansworth
Herts
WD3 4DU

Copyright © Beth Appleby 2025

British Library Cataloguing-in-Publication Data

A catalogue record for this book is available from the British Library.

This book and all other Instant Apostle books are available from Instant Apostle:

Website: www.instantapostle.com

Email: info@instantapostle.com

ISBN 978-1-912726-90-5

Printed in Great Britain.

Disclaimer

While this is a true-life story, the events are recounted from the author's point of view and memory. No recordings were taken of the consultations and conversations, so no speech included is directly quoted but has been written by the author to illustrate the experience remembered. Every effort has been made to present a well-balanced view, and some names have been changed to ensure anonymity.

Some diary entries and social media posts have been lightly edited for the purpose of this book.

In loving memory of Rowena

Contents

Foreword 13

1. Where it all began 15

2. Waiting 20

3. Before the diagnosis 25

4. The phone call 30

5. Dealing with the diagnosis 34

6. Silent scan 39

7. Grief 46

8. Hannah 50

9. Announcement 55

10. Appointments 60

11. Gabriel 65

12. Early Christmas 69

13. The neonatologist 75

14. Calling the hospice 80

15. Questions 84

16. Stillbirth is still birth 88

17. Naming 91

18. Every Life Counts 96

19. Another scan, another opinion 100

20. Yorkshire Christmas 104

21. New Year's Eve 109

22. The specialist 113

23. Early January... 121

24. Baby clothes... 126

25. Late January 129

26. MDT 133

27. Instagram post... 138

28. Nightmare 140

29. Early February.. 148

30. The hospice.. 153

31. Final scan 158

32. CTGs 162

33. Birthdays 165

34. Birth 169

35. Aftermath.. 175

36. Hospital: Day one... 179

37. Hospital: Week one 183

38. The geneticist... 192

39. Hospital: Week two 197

40. Home... 205

41. Adjusting... 211

42. Spring.. 220

43. Living with Hope... 224

44. Future hope 230

45. Feedback meeting... 236

Postscript: Writing 246

Acknowledgements... 251

For everything that was written in the past was written to teach us, so that through the endurance taught in the Scriptures and the encouragement they provide we might have hope.

(Romans 15:4)

Foreword

It was a prayer meeting I will never forget, and in fact, it was the best one of my life. Months of praying for Beth and Paul through their dire diagnosis and courageous response culminated in an impromptu zoom prayer meeting.

We prayed for strength for Beth and the family, for hope against all hope, for life. We strained together, summoning all the grit and hope and faith we could muster, to see God's purposes birthed in and through this family tragedy. We prayed for the skills of the doctors and ultimately the skill of the Great Physician Himself – a God whose name is higher and strength is greater than disease and even death itself.

I had one eye on the computer screen and another eye on my phone, where prayer updates were being posted.

My phone pinged, and I looked down at it and gasped.

I will never forget that moment; that photo. We all dissolved into floods of tears.

I first met Beth when I had just relocated to the UK. We took walks together as she shared her stories of life as a missionary in Cairo. At that time, I thought to myself, 'you've got to be gutsy and full of grit to be a single female missionary in Egypt.'

And she is. Gutsy. Full of grit. Full of grace.

One of the most striking things about Beth's story is that she refused to let anyone write the narrative of her life. She strove to find herself in God's story, to allow God's word alone to define who she was and the nature of the story she was part of. Again and again, as people spoke words of death over the fruit of her womb, she looked to heaven. She understood that God alone is her chief orienting reality. She shared the conviction of

Elizabeth, another woman in the Scriptures who experienced a miracle pregnancy and birth, that 'No word from God will ever fail' (Luke 1:37).

It takes a lot of courage to believe, really believe for the best, but at the same time plan for the worst. Beth's faith wasn't starry eyed, dislocated from earthly realities. She looked death in the face, planned and prepared for it, but ultimately put her faith in the God who said, 'I am the way, the truth and the life.'

This book is an essential resource and companion to those navigating perilous journeys. Beth shares her personal and painful story with vulnerability and courage. As a seasoned traveller in previously uncharted and perilous territory, she's now a wise and trustworthy guide, ultimately pointing us towards the God of all hope.

Jill Weber, Global Convener of the Order of the Mustard Seed and author of 'Even the Sparrow'

1
Where it all began

2nd November 2021

There is an arrogance in continued good health, an assumption you'll always be well (old age permitting some frailty, of course), and two straightforward pregnancies had given me a misplaced confidence that all would continue to be well.

I was a stay-at-home mother of two preschoolers, Martha, who'd just turned four, and Jamie, who was almost two years old, having taught English abroad before getting married. I had taken my previous two pregnancies and births for granted, and although I knew of friends who had experienced complicated pregnancies and even baby loss, I was naive and had thought none of that would ever affect me.

In fact, I felt so assured and relaxed in our third twenty-week scan, I almost asked the sonographer how often she had to tell parents something was wrong. I'm glad I didn't. Noting she was quietly concentrating, I decided to leave her to it, thinking it was best not to disturb her. We were running behind schedule because the baby had been tightly curled up when we'd first been called, a rather unaccommodating position for a scan. After leaving to eat, drink and move around, we were back, and thankfully the baby was now awake and active.

The twenty-week scan for the vast majority of parents is considered the gender scan, as they can find out if they're expecting a boy or a girl. Oblivious to all the things that could be seen as 'abnormal', they sail in and out of the room, clutching new scan photos and planning the announcement of their baby's gender on social media.

The twenty-week scan for the medical world is more accurately called the anomaly scan, as its main purpose is to check if the baby is developing correctly and if there are any abnormalities. We'd been so confident in our second pregnancy that my husband, Paul, a GP, hadn't even attended the scan, instead remaining in the car with our napping baby. This time round, he'd almost not made it again due to work commitments, but he'd managed to wangle a few hours out of the day to join me. I'm extremely grateful he did.

I had no indication until the end of the scan that anything was amiss. As she finished up, the sonographer turned to me and said she had found a few concerning things.

'The baby's bowel is showing up as echogenic, which means it looks white on the scan like bone, rather than grey like flesh. This is not uncommon and could mean you had a small bleed in early pregnancy and the baby swallowed some of that blood and that's what we're seeing on the scan. Or it could mean something a bit more serious. Also, the baby seems to be small, below the fifth percentile. Again, this might not signify anything, but because your previous two babies were of average size, and taking the echogenic bowel into consideration, it's best you see a consultant as soon as possible.'

We were stunned. Something could be wrong and nothing could be wrong? We struggled to make sense of it.

'It's best not to google anything and wait until you see the consultant. Would Thursday morning work for you? You'll be offered some blood tests then too, to rule out things like infections and genetic conditions, so you might not have any answers for a few weeks.'

I was grateful we didn't have a long wait until the next scan and Paul was available that morning without having to rearrange his work day. Of course, there was no question now of him not accompanying me.

The peace and complacency of a straightforward pregnancy was shattered. Uncertainty crept in; worry followed.

'What if this is nothing?' I asked Paul on our way home. 'What if she made a mistake, or these things don't signify anything?'

He was quiet, digesting the information and scanning his medical knowledge for clues, desirous not to scare me or jump to any conclusions.

It did not help that he then had to return to work for a few more hours, and we were unable to process together any more until late in the evening.

'Was everything OK?' my mother asked as I entered the house and relieved her of childcare duties.

'Uh, actually, they're slightly concerned the baby is a bit small so they want us to see a consultant on Thursday morning.'

'Oh, OK. What are they worried about?' she queried.

'We don't know right now; they need to take blood tests to rule things out.' I fudged a response, not wanting to worry her or give any answers we didn't have.

My foremost feeling right then was gratitude for my children. They were playing happily together, totally unaware our happy little world had just been shaken. I felt wonder begin to bloom as the details of their healthy bodies became more vivid – their fully formed arms and legs, the intricate system of life inside. The day-to-day difficulties of motherhood dissolved as I realised how fortunate I was to have them.

Still, I found myself haunted by these two extremes for our new tiny baby: something significantly wrong or nothing wrong at all. Which was it to be?

The decision to have a third child had not been clearcut. While I enjoyed and appreciated having my children, I had struggled with pregnancy, birth and breastfeeding.

Morning sickness (a misnomer) was far worse than I'd expected – it affected my every waking moment for three whole months and felt more like food poisoning with constant nausea, aching limbs, headaches and extreme exhaustion. Some days I felt so unwell, I could barely make it from bed to bath and back again. Being in my late thirties, with a body impacted by previous pregnancies, meant I struggled with carrying another growing little human. Pelvic pain made it hard to stand for long, walk far, carry my toddler or push a pram – quite crucial things when you already have little kids! Also, I had never found breastfeeding easy to establish, requiring a substantial amount of time and support.

At this stage, our lives felt settled and manageable as we'd got past the intense baby phase and were in a good routine with preschool and playgroups. Our nights were mostly unbroken and I felt loath to disturb that peace. COVID-19 lockdowns and restrictions were easing, which meant a return to normality – and yet, deep down, I had a nagging feeling our family wasn't complete. We were missing another little person, but could I go through it all again? I wasn't sure I could handle feeling so ill in early pregnancy that I struggled to take care of my children. Combine that with the discomfort of late pregnancy chasing around a toddler and preschooler, the nights you wonder if you'll ever sleep again because they tag-team wake-ups, and the difficulties breastfeeding… I wasn't sure I had it in me! If I could go through it, however, the benefits would be well worth it: we would have another unique little person to raise, get to know and love.

I knew I had to make this decision quite quickly, or the decision would make itself over time.

It was Easter 2021 while I considered these thoughts, and part of the Easter story came to have significant meaning. Having been raised in a Christian home, I believed in God and decided to follow the teachings of Jesus from a young age. My faith has only grown deeper as an adult, finding the Bible very fresh and relevant to my life and experiencing the closeness of God in the good times and the bad.

In the Easter story, before Jesus is arrested, He goes to a quiet place with His disciples to pray and He wrestles with a decision He has to make. Can He endure the pain, shame and humiliation of execution on a cross, knowing it would pave the way for the salvation of anybody who believes in Him as Lord and Saviour? A brief but hugely intense period of suffering for Him, to achieve redemption for humankind? He would face false accusations, flogging and a slow and agonising death in full public view. It was horrendous to contemplate. What He would achieve, though, would last for eternity, set captives free and change the whole course of history.

While I would not equate my suffering with Jesus', it gave me a framework in which to make the choice, with a deep sense of peace. Pregnancy, birth and the newborn period might seem like hardship for me, but it would be extremely brief in comparison to the lifetime of a human being. The glory of having another child to see grow up and develop and blossom into their own incredible personality would far outweigh what I anticipated going through.

This would be the first of many times a story in the Bible shaped our response and gave us a framework on which to hang our understanding of what we were going through. One phrase from a verse talking about Jesus, summed it up for me: 'For the joy that was set before him he endured the cross' (Hebrews 12:2).

For the joy set before me, could I endure my cross?

Yes. I decided, yes. Little knowing that the shape of our suffering would look vastly different from my expectations: far more intense and with a much greater impact on our families and communities than we could ever have imagined.

2
Waiting

3rd-4th November 2021

What is worse: knowing or not knowing? Knowing something bad is about to happen, or being blissfully unaware? Knowing what you're dealing with so you can prepare for it, or the uncertainty that allows your brain to supply worst-case scenarios and imbues the darkness with hideous monsters, scarier unseen than seen?

The next morning I'd woken up very early and was unable to get back to sleep – it was the start of night wakings where the brain processes all it can't during the day because you're too busy to let it ruminate. I had complied with the sonographer's instructions to steer clear of Google at this point, sure it would provide more questions than answers, as I clung to the possibility it was all nothing and just an unpleasant scare.

I started to wonder if the baby's small size was my fault because I'd been trying to watch my weight this pregnancy and not have quite so many pounds to lose after birth. Or was this all due to an infection I'd picked up and passed on? Had I not been careful enough?

I wondered if we might have to wait until the end of the pregnancy before getting answers, if it was something only detectable after birth. That felt like a lifetime away, enduring the strain of pregnancy and with a potentially heartbreaking outcome. Also, would this all result in birth being affected – would it mean an early induction or even a C-section? I'd had quick, natural labours with the other two and had planned for a home birth this time, in case there wasn't time to get to the hospital.

Were there more complications that hadn't been picked up yet? More serious ones?

I took a long nap that afternoon while Martha and Jamie were out with my parents, deeply grateful for their help and support so I could rest. In my time alone, I tried to have realistic expectations for the scan the next day. It was unlikely we'd learn anything new until all the blood tests had come back and I knew that could take a while. Deep down, I hoped the consultant would negate all the sonographer had said and come up with a reason why these two concerns could prove to mean nothing at all.

The following day, we sat in the waiting room for an hour before we were seen: an hour to sit with our fears and worries and feel the stress levels rise.

I'd been trying to remain in a place of peace, trusting that God knew exactly what was wrong and we would soon have reassurance, but this waiting was tough. I could no longer avoid the thoughts I'd managed to keep at bay, and the black shape of the unknown in our future taunted me.

Other couples came and went, emerging from the main scan rooms joyous and excited to now be able to share their news.

Another lady sat alone, having arrived before us.

'Have you checked in with the desk?' I asked her. 'You've been here longer than us and we've sat here for almost an hour!'

'Oh, I'm here for Dr Richards,' she replied wearily. 'She always runs late,' indicating a door further up the hallway.

'That's who we're seeing too,' I told her, realising with dismay we'd have to wait for her to be seen first, giving us even more time to sit with our fears.

It felt cruel to be left for so long, with all the questions and uncertainty, unable to distract ourselves. I envisioned this scenario as a circle of Dante's hell – the unending torment of not knowing what's to come, for good or ill.

Eventually we were called in, with an apology detailing a previous scan with a set of twins who had a lot of complications.

I lay on the table again, belly out and gel squirted on, waiting for the expert opinion as Dr Richards swept the ultrasound probe over the bump.

The echogenic bowel and small size of the baby were confirmed.

'What I don't see,' she was able to tell us, 'are any markers for conditions like Down syndrome, which would include abnormalities like a hole in the heart, curled up fingers, a missing nasal bone and so on. That doesn't mean we can rule it out. We'll only find out though a blood test or an amniocentesis.'[1]

She showed us white debris floating around in the amniotic fluid surrounding the foetus, which she assumed was what the baby had swallowed, causing the bowel to look white on the screen.

'The baby does have short "long" bones, that is the bones in the arms and legs, which can be a marker of genetic conditions. Although you both aren't exactly tall, so it might just indicate petite stature. Now you need to decide whether you want to have the tests and see if we can find out what's going on, or if you'd prefer not to?'

We knew the doctor had asked this question because we hadn't taken the combined screening test at twelve weeks, which gives a percentage likelihood of the baby having conditions like Down syndrome by taking a measurement of the fluid at the back of the neck as well as a blood test. My refusal wasn't due to any strongly felt principles but to an encounter a few years previously. I'd not felt well enough in my second pregnancy to go to the doctor's surgery solely for that blood test, and had assumed anomalies were usually obvious by the twenty-week scan anyway.

---

[1] An amniocentesis is an invasive test offered during pregnancy, where a needle is inserted into the womb to collect some of the amniotic fluid. It can carry a level of risk to the baby.

Then when I had gone for the dating scan in that pregnancy, the sonographer noted I'd not got any results from the blood test and I explained I'd cancelled the appointment, feeling too unwell to walk to the surgery pushing a toddler in a pram up the hill to get there. She offered to have the test done in the hospital and I thought, 'Why not?' and agreed to have it done right then and there.

I wish I hadn't.

The screening coordinator who took my blood wasn't in a great mood and proceeded to ask how many weeks I was. When I told her, I then received an unwelcome lecture about the timing. The coordinator implied I'd left it late to make a decision about terminating the pregnancy if any of the results came back as high risk.

I found it shocking and deeply offensive.

I believe that God grants life and all life is a gift, and so I have never considered termination would be an option for us. I am aware that having a child with complex medical needs can be more challenging than those with non-disabled children can ever imagine. Yet these children and adults are still loved and can teach us so much about life, love and joy.

I didn't voice any of this, being a non-confrontational type (especially with people I do not care for and never expect to encounter again), and vowed not to take that test the next time.

So now we found ourselves in a situation where the medical staff thought we didn't want to take tests out of principle and assumed we might opt out of further testing. I tried to explain I hadn't wanted to know that early as it wouldn't have made any difference to us continuing the pregnancy.

All of my past experiences and assumptions dissipated as I was faced with the reality of what lay ahead. Declining the amniocentesis because of the small risk of miscarriage, we explained we did want any non-invasive tests to be able to prepare.

'One of the tests is called the NIPT test, which stands for non-invasive prenatal testing, and it checks for genetic conditions like Down syndrome. Another test is to see if you're a carrier of cystic fibrosis,' Dr Richards continued. 'If you are a carrier, then we'd test Paul as well to see if he is. If you both are, and everything else comes back negative, then we would test the baby at birth – we wouldn't know for sure until then.'

I had heard of cystic fibrosis but didn't know anything about it. Might this be the diagnosis that would shape our family's future and become a daily reality for us?

As we headed home, my thought process at this stage was, 'OK, a disabled child, we can do this. Paul is medical and I can stay at home to be their carer... I know it'll be really tough and take a lot of my time, but maybe this is the cross I'm to bear and I'll love this child.' I leaned my head back and closed my eyes, holding back the tears that were threatening.

'The children,' I wondered. 'How will this impact them? My time and attention will be split so much more than I imagined.' The thoughts flooded my mind in quick succession and I felt anxiety rise. I tried to slow my breathing as I fought to reassure myself and focus on being thankful for my medically trained husband, my family support unit and my active church community. I wouldn't be doing this alone.

I wrote this passage in my diary that night:

> When you pass through the waters,
> I will be with you;
> and when you pass through the rivers,
> they will not sweep over you.
> When you walk through the fire,
> you will not be burned;
> the flames will not set you ablaze.
> (Isaiah 43:2)

3
Before the diagnosis

5th-10th November 2021

We had no more answers than before meeting the consultant and now we had a timeline to wait out – a week for the first set of blood test results and potentially up to two weeks before we had any clear, concrete answers.

Paul was confident. 'There'll be nothing wrong with this child. All the results will come back clear. I'd be very surprised if anything comes back positive.' I leaned on his faith but remained sceptical, wondering if my world was about to be changed beyond recognition.

The next day was Bonfire Night[2] and we have a tradition of watching fireworks as a family from our loft room. There we have a clear view west and east and run back and forth between the two windows, looking for the next display to be started in neighbours' gardens or local parks. Over the years, we have discovered that staying home is much easier than standing around in the cold and rain with small children!

During the day I'd taken Martha to an ophthalmologist appointment at another hospital to check her eyes, and when I was told the doctor couldn't see anything wrong at all, I hoped and prayed that might be the case for her baby sibling as well. I prayed the words, 'May there be nothing wrong at all!'

I'd been having stomach cramps after a tummy bug and felt concerned enough to phone the Pregnancy Advice Line – a

---

[2] Also known as Guy Fawkes Night, it is an annual celebration in the UK involving fireworks and bonfires.

service I'd not called before, but soon became a frequent user of. The midwife answering was able to reassure me pain across the belly rather than lower down in the abdomen was probably stomach cramps rather than labour, and therefore nothing to be worried about. Where I'd usually been relaxed about the odd ache and pain, now all my symptoms were magnified and became causes for concern.

It was the same week that I'd been asked to give my first talk at our recently established church – awkward timing. I was grateful I'd prepared in advance so there wasn't too much more work to be done, as now, understandably, my focus was entirely elsewhere. I'd been asked to speak on the third chapter of James, a letter named after its author, which talks about the need to be careful with your speech because words are powerful. It states, 'the tongue is a small part of the body, but it makes great boasts. Consider what a great forest is set on fire by a small spark' (James 3:5).

One excellent speaker I'd watched to prepare, Tim Keller, said this: 'Words create reality.'[3] God created the world by speaking it into existence (Genesis 1). We can make or break relationships, situations, reputations and others' self-esteem simply with our words. I had no idea how scarily true this would soon be for us. Not only would a doctor's words radically shape our reality in the imminent future, but we'll never know how much the words of prayer also defined our family's future.

While I had refrained from researching the symptoms for the days between the first two scans, after my talk was over and my mind was free, I knew I couldn't wait two weeks for the results. I turned to Google.

Fetal growth restriction (FGR) was the one definite diagnosis we had, meaning the baby in the womb was smaller

---

[3] Sermon by Rev Timothy Keller at Redeemer Presbyterian Church on 3rd January 2010. Available at www.oneplace.com/ministries/gospel-in-life/listen/a-community-of-peace-making-881039.html (accessed 12th December 2024).

than expected for its age.[4] I remembered the consultant had talked about short long bones, so I looked that up too.

I read a lot of articles and studies that day, but one stuck and deeply impacted me.

It was titled 'Outcome of fetuses with short long bones'[5] and included seventy cases from August 2005 to October 2013. The objective was 'To study the outcome of fetuses with short long bones seen during any period of gestation' and the results shook me to the core.

Other than twenty-nine terminations, the results listed 'four intrauterine deaths, two neonatal deaths, two stillbirths'. I was stilled with shock and horror as I digested this: four babies died in the womb, two died shortly after birth and two were born sleeping. The words were seared in my mind. I could barely breathe. It gradually sunk in that we might not be dealing with a disability but with a death. I shut my laptop as if by shutting it I could make the information disappear.

'Please God, no. Let my baby live.' I found myself praying without conscious thought.

'Let my baby live' was to become a refrain I would pray as a breath prayer – a prayer you pray so regularly that it becomes like breathing, or a refrain you pray as you breathe in and as you breathe out.

Breathe in: Please God. Breathe out: Let my baby live!

That night, our eldest had an unsettled night with a sore tummy and a headache, and we were in and out of bed attending to her. I tried to keep the feelings and worries in and press it all down, but there's something about the silence and darkness of the dead of night during which you can't hide and pretend any more. After the third wake-up, around 4am, it all caught up with me and I couldn't hold back tears. The reality that our baby might die was so stark and so horrific, I couldn't stop crying.

---

[4] Any baby under the tenth percentile is defined as having FGR.
[5] fetalmedicine.org/abstracts/2014/abstracts/450.pdf (accessed 12th December 2024).

Paul, concerned for my health, asked if I was in pain, and I explained to him my new worries and fears. It seemed that, being medically trained, he had already known what I had only just discovered. I felt sorry he had kept it to himself, attempting to shield me from potentially unnecessary grief. He had also wanted to keep positive and not assume the worst before we had any results back. I was grateful for his comfort as we hugged and prayed together, feeling helpless.

At the same time, it felt like I was overreacting, catastrophising and jumping to conclusions. I hadn't a clue what having a genetic condition really meant, or its potential impact on life expectancy, and previously had no idea that death could be a potential outcome.

In the morning, I found the study again to send it to Paul and noticed it was conducted in India – a country with significantly higher infant mortality rates (almost ten times higher in some states) than the UK.[6] I tried to reassure myself there might have been other factors at play and our case could be very different.

I phoned the screening team in the Maternity Unit at the hospital to talk about the likelihood of a stillbirth, and the midwife was able to explain they kept a close eye on any babies they were concerned about. If the baby stopped growing or if the blood flow to the placenta seemed to be affected, then the advice given was usually for the baby to be delivered.

'Oh, OK,' I replied. 'All of my babies have been born late, at forty-two and forty-one weeks, so I'll have to get my head around that.'[7] A new reality was slowly starting to dawn – that this pregnancy might take an alternative route to my others, but we still didn't know the full picture.

We started to tell family and friends something might be wrong with the baby, that we were waiting on test results and

---

[6] www.cia.gov/the-world-factbook/field/infant-mortality-rate/country-comparison (accessed 12th December 2024).

[7] Forty weeks is a full pregnancy, with more than thirty-seven weeks being classed as full term and less than thirty-seven as premature.

were trusting it would all be fine. We had refrained from sharing because it was all still so unknown and we had no concrete answers to give; however, we'd always tried to be open and valued sharing the journey with our community.

During a time of sung worship at an event, a friend, Andrea, offered to pray for me and I burst into tears. She had been through a similar situation a few years previously when she and her husband, Peter, had had a scare at their first twenty-week scan and hadn't known the baby was fine until she was born.

As she prayed for me, I knew she had been in my place and could understand the pain and worry in the uncertainty. I still felt like I was overreacting when I felt safe enough with her to whisper the words, 'I don't want the baby to die.' It still felt a ridiculous thing to fear, as if the possibility was an unimaginable extreme. How sheltered I'd been!

4
The phone call

11th November 2021

We'd been told the first set of results would come back after a week and it was now exactly a week later. Between my first and second pregnancies, maternity care in my local area had transitioned from paper to digital and I now had an app I could check. Which I did, constantly. As the day wore on, I convinced myself I wouldn't hear anything until the next day, and tried not to think about it.

Paul was on late duty that day, working until 8pm and returning after the children were in bed. After picking up Martha from preschool, I took her and Jamie to the nearby supermarket, arriving home an hour later, laden with bags and physically exhausted. I set the kids up in front of the television and carried the bags to the kitchen. I was just starting to unpack when the phone call came.

It was 4.30pm, and the words delivered over the phone were about to change my life.

'Hello, is this Beth? This is the screening coordinator at the hospital.'

I recognised who she was and couldn't believe we were interacting again. My desire for news overrode all past prejudice.

'Is this a good time?' she asked.

I wonder if she'd called me straight away when she got the results or if she'd paused, working out exactly what to say and how to say it. Or had she procrastinated for a while, delaying the delivery of news no one would want to give?

'If you've got results, I'd like to hear them.'

'Do you understand what the NIPT test was testing for?'

'Yes,' I replied, genuinely thinking I did and wanting to get straight to it.

The initial blow was dulled by ignorance.

'You've come out as having a high probability of Edwards' syndrome or Trisomy 18. Actually a 95 per cent chance.'

My world stopped. We'd got a positive result, but I had no idea what it was or what it meant. We'll definitely have a baby with a severe disability?

'Mummy! Mummy! Jamie wants to watch this, but I don't want to!'

'But Mummy, it's my turn and I get to watch what I want to!'

Their voices broke into my stunned silence and my world started turning again. It had to. As a mother, it couldn't stop.

'Wait a minute, please!' I pleaded with my children. 'I'm on an important call.'

'But Mummy, Mummy, Mummy!' their voices chanted, insistent and loud.

'Is there a better time to talk?' the voice on the phone gently asked.

'No, no, I need to know now. But maybe give me a few minutes to sort my kids out. Can I call you back straight away?'

We hung up and I tried to find something both children were happy to watch. I felt intense frustration as they disagreed; the knowledge of what was affecting our baby was just within my grasp, if they'd only settle.

I phoned back as soon as they were quiet and asked what Edwards' syndrome was and what it meant for my unborn child.

'It's so rare, I'll have to read the information to you if that's alright?'

The coordinator proceeded to explain that Edwards' syndrome is a genetic condition similar to Down syndrome where the baby has an extra chromosome. The words came in a blur and I couldn't take much in. Halfway through the reading, all I wanted to do was end the conversation and get on to Google so I could work it out myself.

I expect the information read aloud explained babies with Edwards' have a short life expectancy and many don't make it to birth alive. It probably said those who are born alive have complex medical needs and their lives tend to be numbered in days or weeks rather than months or years.

What I do remember from the conversation is a name whirling slowly into my consciousness: Hudson.

Friends of mine in America had had a baby with Trisomy 18 – they knew before he was born and he had lived for eight and a half hours. They celebrate his life on his birthday every year and I remembered their slogan: 'Celebrate Hudson'. Eight and a half hours of life… it was all I could think about.

'We do need to decide next steps.' I snapped back to the conversation. 'You could go to a specialist hospital for a thorough scan and invasive tests to confirm the diagnosis or not. You will need to see the consultant soon, though, as you'll need a new plan of care.'

'It all changes from here,' I thought.

I wish I'd paused when the phone call ended and not rushed ahead to call Paul at work. I wish I'd had the emotional strength to hold off for a few minutes to work out what would have been best for him. I wish I could have thought through if he needed to know right that second, if the news could have waited and been delivered in person; if I could have given him the chance to actually digest it, rather than have to plough through another few hours at work with the diagnosis on his mind and the knowledge his wife was distraught at home, with two preschoolers to put to bed.

Instead, I didn't pause to reflect; I was bursting with the news and felt I had to tell him, right then and there. I phoned him at work.

'Paul, the screening coordinator has called with results. It's Edwards' syndrome. The baby might not live.'

I cried so hard it made the children cry.

I knew in that moment I needed to put them first; I needed to calm down and comfort them.

'Sorry, Paul, I've got to go, I've upset the children. We can talk later.'

'Why were you crying, Mummy? What's wrong?' Martha wanted to know.

'Something's wrong with the baby, that's why I'm sad.' I tried to explain in a way they'd understand but wouldn't cause too much concern. 'But don't worry, I've calmed down now. What do you want to watch next?'

I am deeply grateful that one of my closest friends, Georgina, was soon due to arrive to help me while Paul was at work. She turned up at the door, like an angel sent from above, with eggnog lattes and Christmas sandwiches and she stayed until after Paul had returned. Never has food been so gratefully received and company been so appreciated.

I don't fully remember what Paul and I talked about that evening. He'd done some research at work and therefore had a good idea what we were dealing with. I told him about Hudson. We wondered together how to tell our families and our church and work communities.

I do remember feeling heartbroken at the thought of never having the bond of breastfeeding again and never having those newborn cuddles. I sat with those feelings for some time: the grief of unmet desire. They summed up for me the most immediate sense of what we were losing. I couldn't think any further ahead than that. It was too painful to consider.

5
Dealing with the diagnosis

12th November 2021

It was time to tell our families. Trying to catch my brother before he started work, we video-called him and my parents to break the news to them before the kids had breakfast. It was challenging. Talking over the noise of small children is always tricky – I was trying to make porridge, Martha and Jamie were clamouring to play games, my brother had to leave for a meeting and my parents said they couldn't hear me very well. At least now they knew the reality we were dealing with, I reasoned. My brother was sympathetic. My parents asked for more information. I advised them to look it up on the NHS website, as I understood the need to research and find out for themselves, even if the answers they sought would be devastating; the opposite of what they'd hoped and prayed for us. I asked them not to tell wider family until we'd had a chance to let Paul's family know.

I had no idea until then how exhausting it can be to have bad news to break; how draining it is to keep explaining the details while dealing with other people's reactions, and how you have to shut down your own feelings to stay present in the moment and continue functioning.

Later on, I went to a church playgroup and told some close friends our news. Steph, a trainee GP, had heard of Edwards' syndrome but had no direct experience, whereas Mallory had. As a nurse in a Neonatal Intensive Care Unit, she had cared for a baby with the condition who had never left the hospital. That was hard to hear. Holly, mother to Ben with Down syndrome, told me her experience. At her twelve-week scan she was told there was a low chance of her son having Down syndrome, but the twenty-week scan revealed a hole in the heart and a missing nasal bone. They were sent to the specialist hospital the following day for an amniocentesis and she described their shock at the prognosis.

My friends were kind and sympathetic. I wondered if I should be more emotional as I shared the news, but somehow I had separated myself from the feelings. It seemed I had to switch off at some level to carry on a conversation, care for my children and try to maintain some sense of normality. It felt as if it wasn't my baby I was talking about, but someone else's; a stranger's baby. Disassociating seemed to be my coping strategy and it became my default in communication.

We told Paul's parents that evening, once the children were in bed. Paul's mother is a nurse and has provided respite care for parents with disabled children. She made it absolutely clear this child would be welcome in our family, and they would give all the support they possibly could. Her response was heartwarming and gratefully received.

That night, we were completely emotionally spent. It felt like our tragic news was an unstoppable stain of spreading black ink that, once spilt, encroached on all of our loved ones' happiness and couldn't be contained.

I cry now, as I write this. Everything I didn't let myself feel then is still there, deep down. The anticipatory grief, the disbelief, the horror at the thought of holding a dead baby – a baby that might never move in this life. As I type, the words unlock the sadness and out it pours, cascading down my cheeks. Emotion cannot be buried alive; it always resurrects.

One discussion Paul and I had at this time was whether we would now find out the baby's gender. We'd found out with the first two because I like to plan, and wanted to have everything ready before they arrived. We had never had that dramatic moment of disclosure at birth where the gender is revealed in the high of hormones and gas and air and utter relief because birth is done. Knowing this was my last pregnancy and therefore our last chance to have that moment, I had previously suggested to Paul we didn't find out the gender before birth. He was fine with that decision, until we got the diagnosis. He told me the day after the phone call he would now like to know the gender so we could choose a name, making the baby more real to him and allowing him to bond with them.

I understood, but I couldn't do it.

Not knowing if I was carrying a boy or a girl kept enough distance for me to not get too attached. If the baby had a gender and a name, then I'd know who we were going to lose; I'd know if my children were going to lose a little brother or sister. A name would add depth to our loss, colouring in images of them missing as they grow up, rather than the current shapeless shadow I had in my mind. I didn't want a face or a name to lose until the time came to say goodbye.

Thankfully, Paul understood and agreed to wait.

That evening, I went to a social with a group of ladies from church and had dinner at a pub with some friends, old and new. I didn't say anything about the baby because I wanted to pretend everything was fine. I wanted to hear all about everybody else's lives and problems to distract me from my own. I found I wanted to pray for others because I didn't know what to pray for myself, other than, 'God, let my baby live!'

The desire for avoidance not only presented itself in topics of conversation where I steered away from talking about the baby, fearing where it would lead; it also presented itself in a great pregnancy pastime: sleeping. The only way to shut out the world and thoughts and fears and the unknown. Physically, I was constantly tired from disturbed nights and the mammoth task of growing a baby. Emotionally, I was drained by grief and by delivering news I would never have believed I'd have to share. I wondered how best to tell people: give some warning that something was wrong, build up to it with a bit of a story, wait until they asked or until there was a natural break in conversation, or bring it up straight away? How much information was helpful to give?

The following day, I phoned a close friend, Rachel, because she was isolating with Covid, and I cried as I told her the diagnosis we'd been given. Paul told his siblings how we were feeling devastated, but also that we still saw this baby as a gift from God and we were determined to appreciate them for however long they lived. Paul sent a vulnerable email to his work colleagues, detailing our situation, and received many caring and positive responses. Other colleagues, however, were open in their amazement that we were choosing to continue the pregnancy.

'You're braver than I would be,' one said.

After a few days, I started to research online and found support groups for parents who'd continued pregnancies with similar diagnoses, and was heartened to discover there are families with living children with Trisomy 18 (T18). Children who'd lived for years! Not only for days or weeks.

Coupled with the baby's frequent movements, I started to hope. What if this baby didn't have full T18, where every cell is affected, but had partial or mosaic T18? I learned that partial meant it was not a full extra chromosome in every cell in the body but part of one, and mosaic meant that only some cells were affected. These babies had a much higher chance of survival and had a huge range of possible outcomes. 'Maybe my baby has one of these,' I tried to comfort myself.

Friends sent messages of support and love, and some dropped round flowers. I fell into a pattern of switching it all off with others and then, when alone, I had two responses. I either dived deep into research online, devouring story after story of people who'd had babies with T18, or desired to forget we were in this situation, devouring anything chocolate-flavoured and distracting myself with light entertainment.

One more unexpected feeling I started to experience, and barely had the courage to acknowledge, was an edge of relief. I felt relief I wouldn't have to suffer through establishing breastfeeding again; relief we'd been saved the nights when you despair you'll ever sleep again; relief at never having to go through weaning again or rounds of teething again; relief at missing out on the season of separation anxiety, where you can't get anything done because their need for you is so all-encompassing. And then guilt and shame, in addition to the ever-present 'normal' mum guilt: guilt at the relief I felt and shame I could ever view my baby passing as at all positive.

Over all of these conflicting feelings of exhaustion and hope and guilt and relief and uncertainty was acute gratitude for Martha and Jamie. I felt deep appreciation for them as individuals, as well as for my already full family with two healthy children. I felt the love and support of our wider family and church community. Even the preschool offered flexible hours so I could leave the kids during important appointments. All of these things spoke of God's goodness and nearness to us, through it all, and I found peace, knowing we were being carried and supported.

6
Silent scan

17th November 2021

This is one of the entries I dread to write. One of the memories I don't want to re-enter.

I delay picking up my diary to read that day. I'm sure I've blanked out a fair amount because I found it so traumatic. Certain phrases are seared on my memory – phrases I've remembered word-perfect after repeating them so many times. Pronouncements of death delivered with no compassion to soften the blow, no kindness or humanity. As I met other parents in our situation, I came to learn this is not an isolated incident but is, unfortunately, heartbreakingly common. We discovered a baby in the womb is not considered a valid baby until it is born, and therefore is treated with little respect or acknowledgement of the worth of its existence.

Anyway, before I get too far into it, let's go back into the day itself.

I had been offered an appointment with another consultant while Dr Richards was on holiday, either on the coming Tuesday at 1pm or Wednesday at 5.30pm. I'd chosen Wednesday, thinking it was easier for Paul not to have to rearrange his work schedule and so it would be easier to go at the end of the work day instead of at lunchtime. On Tuesday, I wished I'd chosen the earlier day because now the wait was prolonged. Even a day felt like a huge amount of time to endure.

Peter and Andrea lived near the hospital and had offered to take Martha and Jamie while we were at the appointment, adding them into their kids' bedtime routine. I thought we had it all worked out so well, forgetting how flexible you have to be with little ones!

Jamie woke up that day with conjunctivitis. Not wanting to repay our friends' kindness with sharing that with their two, I called to cancel and quickly messaged friends without children to see if anyone could come and babysit. As always, our church community came through for us and a lovely lady with grandchildren herself, Rowena, said she could come from teatime until we returned. The children's pastor, Sam, was free to pop in and help too.

We headed to the appointment with hope in our hearts. Surely with only an echogenic bowel and small size, our baby could be one of the Edwards' babies who lived? With no heart condition, surely we had a better chance of meeting our baby alive? If they couldn't find anything else wrong, wouldn't the consultant be optimistic about our chances?

Dr Brown was punctual in seeing us, and I remember admiring the immaculate appearance: the hair was styled perfectly and the outfit was smart, well-fitted and clearly expensively made. A face mask covered the lower part of the face and I will always curse Covid, not only for stealing lives, incomes and social contact, but for having to receive this news from someone whose face was hidden from me – expressionless and a stranger because of the mask. I was grateful, though, that we were far enough past the initial crisis of Covid that Paul was allowed to come with me. I'd heard of some mothers having to attend scans and receive devastating news totally alone, and of some having to go through the early stages of labour without a birth partner to support them. The poor birth partner had to wait in the car park to get the call saying the mother was far enough along for them to now come in and be present for the actual birth. There definitely were moments, I think, where the health service lost sight of the person in front of them in the fight to stop the spread of Covid.

But I digress; I'm procrastinating writing about this moment. To date, one of the worst moments of my life. Before I launch in, I want to emphasise that this is my memory of the event; I didn't take a recording so have no exact records. A doctor and a patient may have contrasting recollections of a consultation as there can be a huge difference between what is said and what is taken in. A doctor's communication might seem clear to them, but what a patient understands and remembers can be influenced by lack of knowledge and coloured by emotion.

OK… here goes. The scan was conducted in absolute silence and lasted for half an hour.

Half an hour of wondering what they were seeing and hopeful they'd see so little of concern that they'd allow themself to be positive. I was yet to understand how our diagnosis could shape and distort the interpretation of a consultant's findings.

Paul was sat to my left-hand side and I lay on the table in the middle of the room. Dr Brown was to my right, scanning with their left hand, and using their right to type into the computer. The screening coordinator I'd spoken to on the phone was also in the room, as well as another member of staff. I don't remember who she was now, but both of them were stood at the back of the room; as the time wore on, I wondered why they didn't sit down and make themselves comfortable.

As you lie on the table, there is a screen positioned at the top of the wall in front of you, so you can see exactly what the person scanning is looking at. Of course, unless you're trained, few of the images mean anything, and unless it's explained to you, you sometimes have no idea what part of the body is featured, let alone what it all signifies.

When the scan was finished, I got up, wiped the gel from my tummy, pulled my top down and sat on the chair next to Paul, facing into the room and towards the consultant. I tried to focus on keeping my breath steady as I felt the nerves intensify.

We'd been warned Dr Brown could be rather direct, but we were totally unprepared for both the information given and the manner in which it was delivered.

This is what I remember the consultant saying: 'This baby is too small to survive. In fact, I fully expect this baby to die in the womb or shortly after birth. The chest cavity isn't large enough to allow the heart and lungs to fully develop. The baby doesn't seem to have grown since your last scan, and has remained totally curled up and hardly moved at all during the scan. I can see fluid around the heart and there is not much amniotic fluid. The baby's movements have felt different, haven't they? Yes, it's pretty clear to me that we're looking at full Edwards' syndrome, which means the baby is incompatible with life.'

We were in shock, reeling from the damning judgement and the bluntness of delivery. How could this person have got so far along in their career and not learned that all they needed to add were softening phrases like, 'I am so sorry to have to tell you this,' or, 'This is going to be hard for you to hear'? We needed a moment to take it in, as all hope drained away and the future we'd been holding on to splintered and disintegrated in front of us, crushed by these hopeless and desolate words.

There was no moment, no silence or space to catch our breath or even hold each other's hands. Instead, Dr Brown carried on talking, ploughing through the information and on to decisions we would need to make.

'Now, I can see the placenta is enlarged and this puts you at greater risk of pre-eclampsia, so you'll need to be monitored closely. I see you've opted for a home birth, which I guess you've already realised will need to be reconsidered. If the baby lives to full term, you will need to decide when to deliver, as smaller babies don't tend to do well the longer the pregnancy progresses. You will also need to decide how to deliver. A natural birth would have the least impact on you, of course. Having a C-section would be the safest option for the baby, but it would affect the few hours you might get with them.'

Dr Brown kept speaking, presenting decisions we would need to make and alternative scenarios for birth and the levels of care offered to the baby after birth, and I felt submerged. I was drowning in the new information and number of decisions we would now need to make. The consultant didn't give us a chance to say anything, and by the time they'd finished, I was blank. I had no questions because I didn't even know where to begin. My brain had stopped at the phrase, 'I fully expect this baby to die in the womb or shortly after birth,' and now I couldn't process anything more.

I sometimes wish I had recorded what was said at the scan because I know there are things I've forgotten or was never able to take in initially. I also don't know how much of my memory of this encounter was tainted by the fact that Dr Brown reinforced bad news, and so the news and the delivery of it became enmeshed and I couldn't distinguish which was dragon and which was breath.

The consultant explained an amniocentesis might carry greater risk for us because of the lack of amniotic fluid around the baby, but reassured us with confidence they would still be able to do it safely. They also told us I would need frequent scans throughout the pregnancy and we could choose to see them or the first consultant we saw, Dr Richards. Although I have a tendency to avoid conflict and a desire not to offend people, I found it easy to state we'd like to continue with Dr Richards.

'We started this journey with her,' I reasoned, 'so maybe we'll continue with her.' Rather than stating the obvious that their difference in manner made it a clear choice. 'No offence,' I added, negating any politeness I'd tried to show.

As we stood up to leave, the screening coordinator expressed her sympathy for us and said, in a way that I expect was supposed to be comforting, a phrase that still haunts me: 'Remember, you can terminate the pregnancy at *any* point up to birth.'

At any point up to birth! The death of my baby was exactly the opposite of all I'd been hoping and praying for, and therefore the last thing I would choose to do. I was equally horrified by the fact I could carry this baby to full term and then decide to end its life as by the fact this was offered as a comfort and reassurance.

Another mother in a similar situation described it well: 'The possibility of termination was so present in these conversations that letting the pregnancy run its course was decisive in itself.'[8]

I remember coming out of the scan numb and overwhelmed, but also feeling like I understood for the first time why someone would opt for a termination for medical reasons. The situation had been painted as so hopeless that it seemed the most logical and even the kindest option to terminate and end everyone's suffering.

There were more than 3,000 abortions performed in England and Wales in 2021 because of foetal abnormalities. Ground E under the 1967 Abortion Act allows a pregnancy to be lawfully terminated if 'there is substantial risk that, if the child were born, it would suffer from such physical or mental abnormalities as to be seriously handicapped'.[9] These consultants hold a lot of power in their words as they explain to expectant parents what life might look like with a disabled child. It all stems from their interpretation of what they are seeing on the screen, and the life of a child is at risk. At no point was it explained to us that there is a margin for error. Truthfully, no one can know what a baby is like or the challenges it might face until it is born. Making decisions about whether they have a right to live or not seems dangerous and potentially disastrous.

Once we had made it clear that termination was not an option for us due to our Christian faith, mercifully it was never mentioned again. I have heard of others in our situation, at different hospitals, who were offered it every time they went in for a scan, which was hugely upsetting for them. Our hospital got this one right.

We rushed home, hoping to get back in time to put the kids to bed. In the traffic, Paul crossed a lane in front of a car he

---

[8] Tamarin Norwood, *The Song of the Whole Wide World: On Grief, Motherhood and Poetry*, London: The Indigo Press, 2024, p23.

[9] www.gov.uk/government/statistics/abortion-statistics-for-england-and-wales-2022/abortion-statistics-england-and-wales-2022 (accessed 12th December 2024).

didn't see whose driver communicated his frustration and anger amply through his horn. I thought, 'If only you knew we'd just been told our baby is going to die…' and vowed to be more gracious to other people's driving mistakes in the future. I could have no idea what they might be going through.

When we got back, it was all quiet, as Rowena had expertly put both children to bed. Steph came round with her husband, James, to give us a beef dumpling stew she'd made for us, and I sat at the kitchen table, eating and eating and eating. Stew and dumplings was the best comfort food I could've asked for right then, and eating was an attempt to fill the void that had been created.

That night I could not sleep.

I was still in shock, horrified by the way our baby had been described, and my head full of all the decisions still to be made, wondering how we would ever make them. When to deliver the baby? How to deliver the baby? What care should be offered if they were born living? Should we have an amniocentesis, or was there no point in subjecting the baby to harm if the diagnosis was already so sure? The consultant's information download and decisions slithered around in my mind like eels I couldn't catch, slipping in and out of my conscious thought and waiting in the shadows of my mind. I knew they were there but I couldn't recall them all to mind, making me concerned I was forgetting important information.

'Our baby is going to die; our baby is going to die,' paraded through my head, unbidden and unwelcome.

I felt shattered, as if my soul had been smashed into tiny, unrepairable pieces, and yet I knew I had to get up the next morning and carry on being Mum, even with the devastation I was now carrying in my soul, with the knowledge of the pending destruction coming to our family.

It was a scenario I would never wish on anyone else, and I pleaded with God to help me survive.

7
Grief

18th November 2021

There is a story in the Bible of a king who loses a baby.

It's actually an unwanted pregnancy, as he sleeps with another man's wife and then arranges for the man to be killed in battle when he finds out this woman is pregnant, so he can marry her himself. It would have been clear this baby was not fathered by the husband, Uriah, as he'd been away at war.

The king, David, is reprimanded by a prophet, Nathan, and warned that disaster will strike David's whole household because of these evil things he has done. Although he is repentant and acknowledges the sin he has committed against God and God relents, there are still severe consequences to his misdeeds. His son becomes ill. Gravely ill.

I remembered this part of the story when sleep was impossible. I looked it up to remind myself of the details and read:

> After Nathan had gone home, the LORD struck the child that Uriah's wife had borne to David, and he became ill. David pleaded with God for the child. He fasted and spent the nights lying in sackcloth on the ground. The elders of his household stood beside him to get him up from the ground, but he refused, and he would not eat any food with them.
>
> On the seventh day the child died. David's attendants were afraid to tell him that the child was dead, for they thought, 'While the child was still living, he wouldn't listen to us

when we spoke to him. How can we now tell him the child is dead? He may do something desperate.'

David noticed that his attendants were whispering among themselves, and he realised the child was dead. 'Is the child dead?' he asked.

'Yes,' they replied, 'he is dead.'

Then David got up from the ground. After he had washed, put on lotions and changed his clothes, he went into the house of the LORD and worshipped. Then he went to his own house, and at his request they served him food, and he ate.

His attendants asked him, 'Why are you acting this way? While the child was alive, you fasted and wept, but now that the child is dead, you get up and eat!'

He answered, 'While the child was still alive, I fasted and wept. I thought, "Who knows? The LORD may be gracious to me and let the child live." But now that he is dead, why should I go on fasting? Can I bring him back again? I will go to him, but he will not return to me.'

(2 Samuel 12:15-23)

Initially I was struck by the final line, 'I will go to him, but he will not return to me'.

I sat up in bed as the tears came and I contemplated the truth that while I would miss my baby terribly on this earth, I would one day be reunited with them, in heaven. I took comfort in the knowledge they'd never know pain or loneliness or fear because they'd be in the place where all tears are washed away and there's no more pain or crying or grief.[10] They'd be well looked after and cared for by Jesus Himself, and when death came for me, we would meet again.

While it did break my heart that I might never be able to be a mother to this dear child of mine: cradle and comfort them, swaddle and soothe them, feed and play with them, I knew this life here on earth wasn't the whole picture. It was not the end of the story.

---

[10] Revelation 21:4.

One day, we would be reunited and we'd have all eternity together: never to feel alone or separated; never to grieve or cry again; being, instead, in the place of perfect love and connection.

'God,' I whispered, heavy with emotion, 'if it is better for this child to go straight to heaven to live with You, then I trust You. You know my heart, You know I want them to live on earth with me, but I release this baby to You now.'

As I calmed down and started to breathe slowly, another aspect of the story stood out to me: David prayed and fasted while the baby lived, and only allowed himself to grieve once the baby had died.

There was a distinct difference between how he held out hope for God to show mercy while there was still life, and his acceptance and grief once the baby had died.

I felt a prompt in my spirit: *Pray while the baby lives and only grieve once the baby has died.*

This became formative in our approach to the remainder of the pregnancy. We decided we were to try to hold grief at bay and, instead, pray, pray and ask everyone we knew to pray!

We did not plan a funeral or dwell on thoughts of our future without them. We tried to appreciate every time the baby moved and communicated to us they were still alive! Every day we had with the baby was prized, and a friend pointed out how in my womb, this little one was in the safest and most comfortable place possible. She felt they knew love on a deep level, were surrounded by safety and the comfort of being home.

I decided grief could wait. I'd have the rest of my life to grieve and miss this baby, and I didn't want to waste the weeks or months we had left together by anticipating life without them.

We were also highly grateful to those who prayed and those who fasted – those who stood with us in our deepest, darkest valley and felt the pain with us, not offering trite answers or glib comfort, but acknowledging just how awful it was.

This was one thing I learned as we started to pass on our news: it is better to say something, rather than nothing. The effort of trying to say something is a comfort, even if your words, as they probably will, fall terribly short of the heartache you want to communicate and the depth of feeling you wish you could translate. As Kate Gross explains in her heartbreakingly beautiful tribute to her twin sons as she faces death from cancer in her thirties, 'The only answer is to say something. There is really nothing you can say that will make things worse, after all.'[11]

If you've never experienced trauma and have no idea what to say, a simple 'I am so sorry' can be enough. It can be helpful to not ask any questions in case the recipient doesn't have the emotional capacity or even the time to respond, or is being inundated with messages and feels too swamped to message everyone back. Try stating something simple like, 'Thinking of you,' and know your friend or family member has probably experienced all of their priorities being reordered and so they won't judge harshly, but will respond with grace to any attempt to connect and express sympathy or comfort. It helps to know you still exist to others and won't be struck off friendship lists because you're not the fun one any more or the fact you might dampen the mood now you're often sad. It can be kind to keep checking in if you can and expressing your love and support without asking anything in return, offering help if you're able. Try not to disappear or say nothing at all, which could increase feelings of isolation.

Over the next few months, I tried to hold grief at bay as much as I was able, yet at the same time, discovered its arrows could pierce suddenly and deeply without warning.

---

[11] Kate Gross, *Late Fragments: Everything I Want to Tell You (About this Magnificent Life)*, Glasgow: William Collins, 2015, p160.

8
Hannah

19th November 2021

I found that any time I was alone, even if that was while walking and pushing Jamie in the pram, the arrows could get through and I would start to cry. Any time I wasn't busy and occupied with the children, the thought of what we were expecting would sneak up on me and implode. With company, I was able to keep my emotions in check and keep it together, but alone, with no one to distract me, I had no barrier against the encroaching sadness.

That evening, Paul was out and I used the time to watch interviews online of parents who'd lost babies with Edwards' syndrome. The screening coordinator had signposted me to two charities that support people in similar situations and I'd been looking at their websites. One is called ARC[12] (Antenatal Results & Choices) and has a lot of useful information on its website, which unfortunately I didn't read. I went straight to real-life stories because I was hungry for happy endings, and then recoiled when all their stories seemed to end in a termination. I found this hard, as everything within me desired for this baby to live, and so, in my highly emotional state, I decided not to look at its website again or access any of the support it offered.

The other charity was called SOFT UK[13] (Support Organisation for Trisomy) and I devoured its factsheets, but also story

---

[12] www.arc-uk.org (accessed 13th December 2024).
[13] www.soft.org.uk (accessed 13th December 2024).

after story of babies born with Edwards' and Patau's syndromes.[14] So many babies lived for too short a time, but there were also stories of children still living, many years old, and I found reading these personal stories gave me something to cling to – a life-preserver thrown into my deep sea of trauma that could keep my head above the waves and stop me from drowning.

That evening, I watched an interview with a couple whose daughter with Edwards' had lived a few precious hours, and they explained how hard they'd had to argue for adequate medical care for their baby. The mother shared how the baby had looked her directly in the eye and how she felt she would have gone through it all over again for that one look. I stopped the video and broke down.

I wept silently, sitting with my head resting on my arms folded on the kitchen table, not wishing to wake or disturb the children. I sobbed and sobbed as I pleaded with God in utter desperation to allow my baby to be one of the ones who lived. All I wanted was for my baby to live – I didn't feel release or guidance from God to pray for healing. I was willing and open to accept a disabled baby with complex medical needs into our family… I just wanted them to live.

There's a story in the Bible of a woman named Hannah who is unable to have children. Her husband, Elkanah, has another wife, Peninnah, who does have children, and she mocks and provokes Hannah because of this. The Bible calls her 'her rival' (1 Samuel 1:6-7) and it records a time when she so provokes Hannah that, 'In her deep anguish Hannah prayed to the LORD, weeping bitterly' (v10).

A later verse reads, 'Hannah was praying in her heart, and her lips were moving but her voice was not heard' (v13), which causes an onlooking priest, Eli, to assume she's drunk. When he

---

[14] A similar genetic condition called Patau's syndrome, T13, which is caused by a different extra chromosome but results in similar outcomes for babies.

challenges her, she answers, 'I am a woman who is deeply troubled. I have not been drinking wine or beer; I was pouring out my soul to the LORD. Do not take your servant for a wicked woman; I have been praying here out of my great anguish and grief' (vv15-16). The story continues happily because 'the LORD remembered her' (v19) and she becomes pregnant with a son she calls Samuel, which sounds like 'heard by God' in Hebrew.

I remembered Hannah and her story as I prayed and wept bitterly and poured out my soul to the Lord, moving my lips but not making a sound. I found comfort in knowing the Lord hears this type of prayer; would He hear mine?

I felt like I'd never be the same person again. This deep anguish and grief would mark and change me.

Earlier in the day, we had received the consultant's report in the post and I'd been shocked to see how far off the scale the baby was in size. Also, the report listed the amniotic fluid as extremely low and I read that to mean the baby wasn't swallowing and urinating, like babies in the womb normally do. In the interview I'd just watched, the parents described how their daughter's oesophagus had not been connected to her stomach, meaning she was unable to swallow any liquid. They hadn't known this until she was born, and I wondered if our baby might have something similar. I'd had extreme thirst in this pregnancy which I hadn't experienced before, drinking pints of water even overnight to relieve it. Was this related? I had no idea, but it felt like it could be.

Two other fears were present that evening: would I get postnatal depression and would our marriage survive?

I'd stood on the edge of the abyss of depression after my first was born as I found exclusively breastfeeding so painful and relentless that I lost all hope of enjoying her as a newborn, and I curled in on myself in my dark, overwhelmed state. I'd thought love meant putting myself through intense suffering for her sake, even if it affected our bonding, and I saw her mainly as a source of demanding need and excruciating pain. In the end we switched to formula feeding, which allowed me space to recover and heal and for others to step in and help, and I found I could develop a close relationship with my new baby.

Having gone there once and mercifully found a way to row back from the darkness and suffocating hopelessness, I knew I was not immune to depression. With no baby to fill my arms after this pregnancy, but only grief and loss to fill my heart, depression seemed a possible and even probable outcome. How would that affect my kids? I stopped that thought process before it went any further, acknowledging the presence of the fear but not allowing it to develop or become too great. There would be plenty of time to deal with it later if need be.

And marriage. There is a lot of strain on a relationship when you've got small children, and a chronic lack of adequate sleep leads to less patience and grace for each other. You find yourself fighting for what you need, not taking time to appreciate your partner's contributions, and left with little capacity to invest in your relationship. I wondered what a bereavement would add to this stew of pressures, and hoped our commitment wouldn't shatter under the weight of it all.

I poured this all out before the Lord, being completely honest and holding nothing back.

Afterwards, I felt calm; like I'd been heard, and whatever the outcome would be, it now all rested in God's hands and I could trust Him with it, like a good judge having listened intently and thoroughly to a trial in court.

In Hannah's story, the priest responds by blessing her and saying, 'Go in peace, and may the God of Israel grant you what you have asked of him.' The passage records how she then 'went her way and ate something, and her face was no longer downcast' (1 Samuel 1:17-18).

I think I experienced something similar to Hannah: not a definite answer for what we'd been asking for, but a deep sense of having been heard. God is a God who hears prayers, even if we don't always get the answers we want (which would be impossible, given how often people pray for conflicting things), but feeling heard and listened to is powerful and uplifting.

You're not being belittled or sidelined, but feel important and significant enough to be listened to, especially when your concern then feels like a burden shared rather than one you stagger under the weight of.

I didn't tell anyone about this time of prayer because it felt sacred, somehow, and private. It was a moment between God and me alone, given structure to and mirrored by a story in the Bible. It was an intimate moment of pure abandoned honesty, vulnerability and connection that wasn't for exposing to other people.

The prayer and weeping had given the dam of emotion an outlet of expression and so released the pressure, for a while.

9
Announcement

20th November 2021

Martha liked to help me push the pram sometimes, and I would lower the handle so that she could reach it easily. She loved doing that even from when Jamie was tiny, and we'd take our time pottering into town to go to a playgroup, bumping him along while he was cuddled up, napping in the carrycot.

As we walked together, the first Saturday after the devastating scan, the pram hit a kerb and she bumped her head on the handlebar.

'I'm OK, Mummy. I didn't cry. I'm brave,' she announced proudly.

'Yes, you were brave, but it is OK to cry when you feel sad or when you get hurt. Mummy cries sometimes,' I replied.

'Mummy will cry when the baby dies,' Martha suddenly stated.

'Yes.' Her declaration had surprised me. 'Yes, Mummy will cry when the baby dies.'

We had wondered how to explain it to the children. Jamie was too young but Martha seemed to understand a lot of what was going on and, I thought, needed to know the truth of what we were facing. Death is often an abstract concept to children, unless they experience a beloved pet dying, so I wasn't afraid to talk about it with her.

The way we approached it was to talk about heaven as the place where Jesus lives now, and where people we love go to when they die. I expect she thought it could be reached on a plane, in the wonderful world of children's logic, yet she seemed to understand when we explained that this baby in Mummy's tummy might not come home from the hospital but might go straight to heaven to live with Jesus. She accepted this, as well as the fact Mummy and Daddy might feel sad and that we still loved her and it was not her job to make us happy again.

Later that day, I managed to briefly join a day of worship. Different worship leaders from the area led an hour each to fill twelve hours altogether and I managed to make one, while Jamie was asleep and Paul read with Martha.

We had told close family at this point but not many friends, and I didn't want to spoil the other attendees' time by sharing our news. There were some people I knew there and some I didn't. I found a quiet corner and spent a lot of time with tears running like rivulets down my cheeks as I listened to the singing and joined in when I could. It was a sweet, sweet time.

I had a very real sense of Jesus coming down to share in our sufferings: as in, Jesus came to earth to live a human life and suffer loss and false accusation and physical pain and betrayal so that He can walk alongside us when we face similar difficulties. He's not removed and pitying us from afar. He is close and empathises with us because He knows exactly what we're going through. How different it is when someone offers comfort or condolences having been through the same experience we have, rather than an emotionally distant onlooker, glad it's you and not them going through this tough time.

As well as this comfort, I had another startling sense that felt like God Himself speaking directly to me: *'I know what it feels like to lose a child.'*

Christians believe God is three in one: one God in three persons, a bit like water can be ice or steam or liquid, depending on the temperature. God the Father allowed God the Son, Jesus, to be sacrificed for our sins, through death on a cross, and so to take the punishment that should condemn us. The Holy Spirit, the third person of the Trinity, is the resurrection power who brought Jesus back from death and is living in us, now and for eternity. We believe God the Father felt the pain of losing His Son, Jesus, even if it was in His plan of redemption for humanity, and knowing resurrection was coming.

'I know what it feels like to lose a child.'

These words floored me and, once again, I wept.

Not only does the God of creation know suffering so as to be able to journey with us and empathise with us, but He also knew the exact tenor of my suffering. He would know the ins and outs and ups and downs of my grief, and how my world would never look or feel the same again.

Later that night I explained all of this to Paul, and shared how this experience could allow us to learn more about the kindness and grace and comfort and goodness of God. If we let it, of course.

Martha prayed at bedtime that night for the baby. One wonderful friend, Mariette, had sent through what her children had been praying for our baby, and the words were so encouraging: one prayed for supernatural strength to come over the baby, another saw the baby being born healthy and strong, and my friend herself saw the baby being formed in a hidden place. The faith of children and the power of their prayers felt a great and glorious thing.

After I explained what our friend's children had prayed, Martha prayed, 'May the baby be healthy and strong and warm and may the baby grow up just like me.'

'Amen and amen,' I whispered in agreement, my spirit holding tightly to her simple yet powerful words.

We were prayed for at church the next day, so then everyone knew.

We'd drafted an announcement for our pastor, Matt, to read out in the service before people gathered around to pray. It read:

> It is with heavy hearts we wanted to let you know that Paul & Beth's baby has been diagnosed with Edwards' syndrome, a rare, life-limiting genetic condition, and has been given a very poor prognosis. Most babies with this

condition die in the womb, and the life expectancy for those who survive to full term is, on average, three days to two weeks. They're obviously heartbroken by this news and their desire is to have this baby born alive to get some precious time with him/her.

They'd really appreciate prayer:

1. for *life* for this baby and the baby to grow. The consultant was extremely pessimistic about the baby's possibility of surviving because it's so small (as there's not space for the organs to develop);

2. for them emotionally, as they navigate the shock & grief of this kind of diagnosis, while needing lots of energy to look after their two wonderful children (who they've never been more grateful for!);

3. for all the tricky decisions they'll need to make about medical care for all the different possible outcomes, which can feel overwhelming and tiring;

4. for Beth's continued good health for the remainder of this pregnancy so they don't have to deliver any earlier than needed.

Please do feel free to send messages to them but know they might not be able to reply to everything. They want to thank everyone who's offered help, prayer and support so far.

What we didn't know was that Sunday was the first time some friends of ours had ever attended the church. Parents of young children, they'd been invited by a mutual friend at a playgroup and, feeling it was rude to refuse, came along. What an intense week to turn up! It turned out to be the start of their faith journey, as they felt they experienced true authenticity and vulnerability as we shared openly about our current situation, as well as witnessing the love and compassion of the congregation as they clearly cared for us and held us in our sorrow.

We also turned to another community to ask for prayer: a network of friends who live abroad and have a high value for interceding for others. They called a day of fasting across the community and, on 1st December 2021, many people refrained from eating any food to focus on lifting up our unborn baby. It was an incredible and powerful act of kindness and solidarity. Many sent encouraging verses, including 1 John 5:14-15:

> This is the confidence we have in approaching God: that if we ask anything according to his will, he hears us. And if we know that he hears us – whatever we ask – we know that we have what we asked of him.

10
Appointments

23rd-24th November 2021

There was a distinct irony to the fact we'd opted for a home birth with our third.

My first two labours had been extremely quick and now we lived further from the hospital, I was worried we'd not make it in time. Jamie's birth had been straightforward and I didn't need (or hadn't had time for) any painkillers other than gas and air and paracetamol. We'd also been discharged from hospital after six hours so it seemed less disruptive to have the baby at home and stay there, rather than risk a stressful rush to hospital and the possibility of me giving birth en route. Of course, all of this was a moot point after the diagnosis because of the expected level of medical intervention the baby would need after birth, as well as the possibility of having a C-section.

Opting for a home birth had meant all of my midwife appointments were conducted at home, which was immensely helpful with two preschoolers in tow. But when we had to change from home birth to hospital care, we were gently informed that our appointments at home would now need to be held in the nearest maternity hub, coupled with the fact I'd now need more appointments to monitor my health. It was an added blow: increased effort and stress at a time I needed less, not more.

The subsequent appointment I already had in the calendar with the home birth midwife was allowed to go ahead, and she had clearly been prepared for this baby to die antenatally. While she was gracious and commiserated with me, I wanted an injection of hope and the possibility of this not ending as badly as the consultant had led us to believe. We listened to the baby's heartbeat and she commented how healthy it sounded, so strong and loud. All other tests were fine, and she also came with some good news.

The senior midwife who headed up her team had given permission for us to continue having appointments at home. She was going to be able to pop in every other week and I wouldn't need to drag my kids to the clinic to be seen. It was a small kindness that made a big difference – allowing us ease and comfort for the appointments rather than adding to our burden.

Later I understood there was another facet to this kindness: the ability to avoid seeing and meeting other pregnant mothers who were having healthy pregnancies and might innocently ask questions about mine. I was grateful to be spared that.

Deciding it was time to let our wider community know, I posted on Instagram that day:

My wonderful little family has received some very sad news...

They say one of the hardest things you can experience in life is the death of a child & it seems we're going to have to learn how to survive exactly that.

Our baby has been given the diagnosis of Edwards' syndrome or Trisomy 18: a genetic condition that is 'incompatible with life'.

The consultant told us, looking at the size of the baby, that it will die in the womb. Even if it did survive birth, the life expectancy would be numbered in hours, let alone days or weeks.

You know what I've learnt since receiving this news?

That you can't keep hope down. We can't stop hoping for life for this baby, even if it's the precious gift of a few hours. That Jesus came to this earth to suffer so He could walk with us through our sufferings. That God the Father knows the pain of losing a child and He grieves with us. That the church really are His hands and feet as we've been surrounded by support, prayer & practical care. That we'll never be the same people again – may we be more compassionate & filled with grace for others as we experience the comfort & nearness of God in a way we never would have otherwise. That as this baby's mother, I can't pray for them to be anything other than they are right now because I already love them so much, I wouldn't want another child in their place. That I'll never take my children & their health for granted ever again. That the valley of the shadow of death isn't the valley of death – death may cast its shadow over this deepest darkest place, but shadows can't crush you. That my cup can overflow with goodness and blessing even while I walk through my worst nightmare.

Please pray with us for life for our baby, for it to grow so the organs can develop, for the amniotic fluid to increase in volume and for my health to not be compromised. Our hearts' desire is for this baby to be born alive & we will need wisdom to know when & how to facilitate that, if we reach that point.

Praise the Lord the baby is alive today! Every day I will celebrate the movements I feel and hope & pray for LIFE!

After posting, I scrolled back through older photos and froze when I came to the photo I'd posted to announce our pregnancy after the twelve-week scan. I'd posted it the day after my birthday, in September, and it showed a scan photo of an outstretched arm ending in a clenched fist with a thumbs up. I'd written, 'Baby no.3 trying to reassure me it's all going to be okay #outnumbered,' and I felt sick. I seriously contemplated deleting the photo, eventually deciding it was part of our story and I didn't need to be ashamed of getting it so wrong.

The next day, I lifted Jamie out of his cot to wake him from his nap, but he was determined not to stir. He snuggled up on me as I sat on the sofa and carried on sleeping. I was then struck by a tragic thought: what if this is the last time I hold a sleeping child of my own? What if I'd wished all of these sweet moments away, never appreciating the closeness and comfort of it because I'd been dreading having to do the newborn phase and survive on so little sleep all over again? Jamie, as a tiny baby, had slept on my chest for the first four weeks of his life – for every nap and even overnight, he was safe and warm on my skin. Eventually, with the aid of a dummy, he was content to sleep in his cot, and slept so well that we kept to his routine strictly, and he only ever napped in the cot or in the car. Had I not appreciated the time he'd slept cuddled up with me at the time because I was worried he wouldn't transition to sleeping by himself, and was the period of co-sleeping now done? Before I was ready? I let him sleep far longer than normal as I tried to enjoy that moment, while also experiencing a wave of grief break and foam in my chest as I contemplated the possible premature end of our baby era.

I joined a Zoom call run by SOFT UK for expectant parents that evening; it was heartbreaking to listen to the stories.

Two couples were at thirty-two weeks of pregnancy and had babies with confirmed full Edwards' syndrome: for one, it was their first and they had conceived through IVF, and the other was expecting their third. Both were girls. One had been told by the larger, better-equipped hospital in their region that they could not transfer their care from the smaller, less experienced hospital because of the baby's diagnosis. They would not offer to prolong the life of a baby with a terminal condition, as it was pretty much seen as a waste of resources. If a child or adult is going to die, why do we fight death with all the available medical expertise and treatments, while a baby with one of these conditions is given up on and denied care? It seemed cruel and unfair.

Even the staff members on the call were personally affected by Edwards' syndrome and I appreciated hearing their stories: Kate had had a baby, Hannah, who had lived for fifty-four days, and Shaun had a little girl with the mosaic version who was a toddler and growing up with no clear developmental delays. Two such contrasting stories, showing the range of outcomes for babies with these types of conditions.

It was hugely beneficial to have the space to share our story and concerns in as much detail as I wanted without having to consider if the listeners were interested or understood. Everyone on the call got it; they knew from experience, fortunately for me and unfortunately for them.

11
Gabriel

I chatted to the mother of a new family at church the following Sunday, as we looked after our kids in the children's group. She had recently lost her father and was open about the pain and grief of it, allowing me space to share our source of sadness.

Not only had she heard of Edwards', but she also knew a family who'd had a son with it and asked if I wanted to be put in touch with them.

I quickly sent her friend, Amy, a message and she offered to meet me for lunch to share stories and connect. This was when I learned about Gabriel.

Her second child, a son named Gabriel, had had a normal pregnancy until a dramatic twenty-week scan revealed multiple holes in the heart, malformed limbs and, like us, a very small size. They kept coming up against almost aggressive bias in the medical world as they held on to hope that he would be born healthy and well. He was born at thirty-seven weeks and lived for a further twelve weeks: half of his life spent in hospital and half at home. Whenever they couldn't stay with him in hospital, people from their church took turns to visit so he was never alone.

After he'd passed and deep in grief, Amy asked God how He could have let this happen and why He hadn't healed Gabriel. She told me of how she'd been lying on the bathroom floor, crying this out, when she suddenly had a vision in her imagination. The twelve weeks of his life played out before her like a film reel and her eyes were opened to see all the times

God had stepped in to prolong his life. God had provided measures of healing and intervention, although not to the fullness they had asked and so longed for.

She prayed for the baby in my womb and was the first one to pray with real faith that the baby would live and be well, rather than only praying for us to have comfort and some time with the baby alive. I shared some of my concerns with her and she responded with encouragement, explaining how her marriage had survived the loss of their son because they both had God to turn to for emotional support and so they weren't solely reliant on the other. They could pour out their heartache in prayer and therefore not lean so heavily on each other that the marriage couldn't endure.

Earlier in the day, I'd been sorting and bagging up the clothes Jamie had grown out of. Knowing we wanted three children, I'd sorted and kept all of the kids' clothes, which were labelled in plastic boxes in the shed. I always found this a tedious task, but that day it made me heart-sick. My hands felt heavy and the clothes mocked me as I questioned whether this was a redundant task if we weren't going to have another child. Were these bags of clothes a twisted joke? I felt a weight in the pit of my stomach. Should I give them away, rather than leaving them in the shed as a terrible reminder of what we weren't going to have? Would I ever be able to summon up the courage to relinquish them, if that meant acceptance of a smaller family than we'd wanted? I was packing up clothes for a boy aged eighteen to twenty-four months, knowing it was highly unlikely our baby would reach that age, let alone be big enough to fit these items. Babies with genetic conditions can struggle to put on weight and are often small for their age. Were these clothes a symbol of what we were never to experience again? It was a truly depressing activity and made me feel awful.

The next day was Jamie's second birthday, and his main present was a giant teddy bear. We'd picked it up in a half-price sale, pushing it in the pram back to the car, much to the amusement of various onlookers. We'd strapped the bear in the back, in-between the two car seats, which the children thought was hilarious and it became the recipient of many cuddles, bandages and well-aimed tumbles.

That night, as Paul had a whisky night with some of his friends, I read through more stories online of families affected by Edwards' syndrome. Sometimes I wanted to delve into research and find out everything I possibly could, as if reading enough stories of T18 babies living might tip the balance in our favour and even outweigh all the stories of babies dying.

As I was reading, a memory surfaced, buried deep and forgotten for a number of years.

The day after our positive pregnancy test for Martha, I'd had a bleed and didn't know whether that meant I'd miscarried or not. Unfortunately, the referral from our GP surgery to the early pregnancy scan team was lost and so after waiting two agonising weeks, I phoned to find out I wasn't even on their system, let alone had an appointment! When I did have a scan, it was gratifying to see the little heartbeat on the screen, although quite weird to see the arms and legs as little nubs that were yet to grow.

That miscarriage scare robbed the joy of the first few weeks of finding out we were pregnant and caused me great concern that the continuation of the pregnancy wasn't guaranteed. Being pregnant can be an emotional trial if you've experienced any kind of baby loss, and even a scare can take away the carefree assumption of all progressing well.

As I had contemplated this one day at a prayer meeting, a thought had come into my head that I believe could have been reassurance from God: *'There is no death in your body.'*

At that time, early 2017, I took it to mean that I could stop worrying about this pregnancy and that the baby would be fine. She was fine. She was now a very imaginative four-year-old who loved princess dresses and singing in the mirror.

Now, almost five years after that moment, I was suddenly reminded of the phrase. This statement of truth and promise: *'There is no death in your body.'*

What did it mean now, carrying a baby with a T18 diagnosis, that there was no death in my body? Did that mean we would not be facing a stillbirth? Could I trust that the baby would be born breathing? How much did I really believe that voice had been an encouragement from above, or was it just a nice thought to reassure myself?

I never settled on a conclusion but I did carry those words in my heart, and hoped beyond hope that they meant life for this baby as much as they had meant life for Martha several years before.

12
Early Christmas

29th November-1st December 2021

We headed down to my parents' home in South Wales to celebrate an early Christmas with them during a week of Paul's annual leave. It was snowing when we left, which felt entirely appropriate, and a little scary on the roads. The kids decided they didn't want to sleep because they were so excited, but eventually dozed off as Paul and I serenaded them with Christmas carols.

The night before, Steph had popped round with forty-eight individually wrapped presents for Martha and Jamie – an incredibly unique and generous Advent calendar for them both. They were delighted each day to find out what their little present would be: a stamp or a book or a sheet of stickers. I could not imagine the amount of time that went into planning, buying and wrapping each of those items!

Our first full day of holiday I spent either in bed napping or on the sofa, wrapped up in a blanket, asking others to fetch whatever I needed. We visit my parents' large bungalow often enough that the kids have their own games and well-worn paths, like the game 'wear Mamgu's (Grandma's) shoes around the house'. I was grateful they were pleased to be there and happy to play independently, and now I had three extra adults on hand to look after the children.

I recorded in my diary I felt 'soul tired': beyond a physical tiredness that can be relieved after a few good nights of sleep. It was more a deep emotional exhaustion from sadness that pulls you down and sucks you dry of all energy or enjoyment of things; a weariness that cloaks you and hangs heavy, dissuading any effortful movement as stillness settles over body and soul. Was this grief? Was I going to feel this for the foreseeable future?

A new variant of COVID-19 had been discovered in the UK, named Omicron, and so we were all back to mask-wearing in public again in an attempt to hinder its spread. I was grateful we weren't in the early days of the pandemic, when we wouldn't have been able to visit at all and I would have been facing this without the physical presence and support of family and friends.

Memories started to surface that had once been sweet and special: Jamie had been four weeks old when we'd had his first Christmas at my parents' house. I felt like I lost much of the celebrations that year between the night feeds, unsettled evenings and the general sense of survival in the haze of post-birth recovery and intense breastfeeding hormones. The memories pinpointed for me all I would be missing out on this time – the newborn cuteness and snuggles as the world narrows down to solely you and them.

A turkey dinner for Christmas lunch has always been part of my family's tradition and holds a special significance for me, after having spent many Christmases in Egypt when I taught English there in my mid to late twenties. While they had been treasured days with special friends, it's not the same as being with your own family, experiencing decades-old traditions. On Jamie's first Christmas Day, he was asleep in the sling and Martha was napping in the pram when lunch was ready. As we ate our turkey lunch, I felt that even if I'd missed a general sense of rest and celebration for Christmas 2019, I had at least had my lunch in peace (even if each mouthful was eaten precariously over the top of my sleeping son's head!).

We had our Christmas turkey lunch for 2021 a month early and it was glorious: perfectly cooked meat, crisp roast potatoes, delicious stuffing, homemade cranberry sauce, oodles of rich gravy and lots of vegetables. My husband is an exceptionally good cook and this meal was one to be proud of. As I experienced a feeling of satisfaction and contentment, I declared, 'Right, I've had my Christmas now. It doesn't matter what else happens in December.' I wanted to safeguard Christmas from being tarred with death.

Abruptly, a bleak realisation hit me and robbed the moment of joy: I am going to hold my baby after they've passed from this life on to the next. I'm going to hold my dead baby. I felt stunned. I didn't know if it was going to be immediately after birth, mere hours afterwards, or if we could have days with them, or even longer. What I did know was that the medical world was preparing for this beloved child to not outlive me. No part of my life could be safeguarded from that.

While we were staying with my parents, we managed a few Zoom calls while they looked after the children. The first was with Hudson's parents, Luke and Hannah, and they told us his story.

They knew he had T18 from fourteen weeks of pregnancy, as a scan had showed up multiple abnormalities: holes in his heart, his bowel outside of his body and a cleft lip. While they prepared for the worst outcome for him, they decided to celebrate every moment of his life and his place in their family.

They told us of the birth, where they had opted for a C-section, feeling convinced it was best for their situation, and at thirty-nine weeks, he was born, not breathing.

It took the medical staff twenty minutes to resuscitate him and Luke shared with us that that was the worst moment of his life: not knowing if this tiny baby would live, and waiting helpless as a bystander to see if he would breathe and they could hold him alive.

This was a sentiment I would hear repeatedly as I got to know more and more families with children affected by T18 or T13 (Patau's syndrome): the absolute uncertainty at birth. There were so many questions – will they be born alive; how long will they live for; are they in pain; will I get to meet them with their eyes open, hold them and communicate some of my love for them?

Hudson did breathe and was held by his loving family every moment of his too-short life. A photographer came to take pictures of them and they shared how much they cherish those photos, while they also provide a stark reminder of how many photos will never be taken of him and how finite the number of them are. Any modern parent has the dilemma of how to store the thousands of photos and videos they take of their darling little children, but for them, no more would ever be taken.

When we spoke, it had been nine years since he had breathed on this earth and they had gone on to have two more children, taking the number of their living children to three. Every year on his birthday, they celebrate him and take comfort in knowing they'll meet again in heaven.

Even after all this time, their love and grief were evident, and he will always remain an integral part of their family. Their living children know about their brother in heaven, and his birth and death day (or anniversary as some call it) will be remembered and celebrated because they are grateful God gave them eight and a half hours to spend with him. Eight and a half hours is the blink of an eye in the length of lifetime you should have with your child, but they had chosen not to become bitter or hardened, but practised gratitude instead.

Their attitude and response continued to shape mine. Instead of fearing what was to come, they gave me a glimpse of what it could look like to appreciate and welcome the little life and the short amount of time we might have with them. As much as I tried not to grieve, the anticipatory grief and sense of loss lurking not far below the surface took on a new hue. Whatever time we would receive with this baby would be a gift and to be celebrated.

That morning, I'd sat and watched the children play in my parents' lounge. Normally if they're occupied and happy playing together, I use the time to read a book or scroll through social media on my phone, or catch up on the never-ending life admin of a parent. I don't pay attention unless there's some crying or an argument clearly brewing. This time, however, I just sat and watched.

They had created a game using a large plastic play kitchen. One of them would pick a piece of fake food and give it to the other, who had an elaborate routine involving the microwave, 'washing' it under the tap, putting it in a pan and finishing it off in the oven. They created a waiting game while it 'cooked', and the non-chef would keep asking, 'Is it ready yet?' Eventually it would be removed from the oven, given to the other child to 'eat', and they would switch roles and the game would repeat. Over and over.

I sat and watched them. Not interfering or asking any questions or suggesting any improvements. Just watched and paid attention, allowing my heart to fill with joy. What exquisite children, happy and content in their little world of imagination and play, and what love I had for them.

It wasn't long before the joy was tinged with sadness as I wondered how many moments like this I had missed because I'd been too busy and had not paid attention. How much of their self-guided play had I taken for granted because I assumed I'd have a lifetime to watch them interact? They were now four and two and their baby years were past, and soon school would dictate our routine. Had I ever really stopped to appreciate it? Had I wished their baby days away because I found the disrupted nights so challenging and now I had no more to come? A whole phase of life had passed me by when I was wishing the time away, expecting to do it all over again and so never fully living in the moment, absorbing it and drinking deep of all its cuteness and joy.

Stories like Hudson's reminded me that these days and phases are a gift and not a given. How much of Martha and Jamie's early years had I wished away and been distracted through as I remained oblivious to how precious they were, how unique and fleeting this season was?

How long the days seem when you're sleep deprived and a tiny person is completely and utterly dependent on you, but how quickly the years seem to fly by, oblivious to how much you want to freeze time and preserve the sweetness of their flavour.

I thought of Hudson and Gabriel many times over the coming weeks and months as I wondered how our story would play out, how long we'd have and how our family would morph to accommodate the loss. Would our family always remain incomplete, missing a whole person from our number while grief took their place at every family gathering, annual celebration and mealtime? Yet also, how much might our adversity provide comfort and a framework for those who came after? Once again, my only option was to trust in God's goodness.

13
The neonatologist

2nd December 2021

I had expectations of a good day because we had pleasant things planned: a visit to the kids' favourite soft play, a Zoom call with a Christian consultant neonatologist, who was kindly speaking to us in his own time, and then dinner out in the evening, just the two of us.

While the day did follow that sequence, it was not a good day.

I hadn't yet realised that I followed a pattern after each devastating consultation where, as time went by, my hopes would rise and I would begin to shrug off negative comments. Each day that passed meant I believed less of what the doctors had said and the movement inside would convince me this baby was faring well.

Knowing that the consultant we'd seen first after receiving the diagnosis was known to be blunt, I associated that with the poor prognosis for our baby and made an assumption that a Christian doctor would surely be more compassionate and caring, and so maybe he would have a more positive message for us. I do think I believed he would tell us a different outcome, so I looked forward to this conversation being more positive, even hopeful.

I'd sent him all of our scan reports so far and he'd looked over them before our call.

He, however, confirmed the baby was too small to survive and I felt my insides empty, slowly draining away to leave me hollow. This wasn't how the conversation was supposed to go!

'I have seen babies with Edwards' syndrome before,' he reassured us. 'They don't have much life force,' he tried to describe to us. 'They don't cry loudly, but whimper, more like a kitten. Their deaths aren't sudden dramatic events but they slowly fade away and stop breathing.'

I didn't want to hear this. I wanted him to tell us the lack of a heart condition was a good sign and the fact there were no major abnormalities, like organs growing outside the body or part of the brain missing, were all factors to lead him to believe this was a baby who would live. His words, even if his manner was more agreeable, echoed and confirmed what we'd already been told.

'I would advise you to prepare for a stillbirth and, if the baby is born alive, for palliative care.'

It was the same message: '*I fully expect this baby to die in the womb or shortly after birth.*'

We were back in the same place: imagining holding a baby born sleeping, or one who barely breathed. I didn't tell him our hopes were dashed all over again and I'd looked to him for some sort of unattainable reassurance that it wasn't going to end with silence and stillness.

We told him we needed to make decisions about when and how to deliver the baby.

'I can't tell you when,' he replied, 'although I can tell you that babies born before thirty-seven weeks struggle, and then you'd have underdeveloped lungs added to the rest of the complications your baby would have. Leaving small babies for longer in the womb, however, has been shown to increase the risk of stillbirth.' It seemed an impossible choice we were facing: deliver too early and the baby would have less chance of surviving; deliver too late and the baby might have no chance at all.

'One thing I want to tell you, though, is the pushback you'll receive if you opt for a C-section. You can elect to have a C-section for any reason in the world and the antenatal teams are happy to give it to you, but as soon as it's for a baby with a genetic condition, there will be questions. The well-being of the mother is prioritised over the baby who isn't expected to live and so natural birth, having less impact on the mother, is preferred. Especially if you've had two natural births before and you've got two children at home to look after, they won't want to give you a C-section. You might have to fight for it.'

Little did I know at that point how accurate and helpful this piece of advice would be and how many times in the coming months I would hold on to it as I experienced exactly what he'd described, while other expectant friends faced no qualms or questions about opting for a C-section.

'It would a good idea to write as detailed a birth plan as you can,' he continued. 'You'll want to communicate exactly how you'd like the birth to go, and what interventions and care you want the baby to receive.'

Again we were faced with the horrifying fact that babies with genetic conditions are not offered the same treatment as babies with a normal set of chromosomes, as if they're not worth the time and expense of treating if they're not expected to live anyway.

He explained we'd need to make it really evident if we wanted the baby to be offered oxygen at birth, which is routine and regularly given to babies who need a little help when born. The range of breathing help available extended up to intubation,[15] which Covid had made a more widely known word in modern vernacular.

'Intubation can be painful, and unfortunately, for babies with these conditions, means there's no going back. It would normally be offered to those who have hope of recovery, giving their body time to fight off an infection, for example, and not as a means to extend life indefinitely.'

Paul, as a doctor himself, understood that you don't inflict harm unnecessarily and so he was nodding along, on board with the concept of intubation being a step too far for a baby with

---

[15] Inserting a tube through a person's nose or mouth to keep their airway open which can be connected to a machine to deliver oxygen.

Edwards', while I still lived in the unknown. How could I know how I'd react if our baby was struggling to breathe and an intervention was being refused? Would I acquiesce quietly, agreeing we were out of options, or would I fight for whatever it seemed the baby needed? Would it be obvious it was the baby's time to go, and so it would be cruel to cause unnecessary pain? I thought that decision could wait.

Writing a detailed birth plan can give a clear indication to the medical team of your desires and wishes, and can communicate for you at a time you might be unable or unwilling to make decisions. It also can be abandoned or amended at any point if you find you change your mind. So I tried to hold it all lightly, knowing my feelings after this baby was born might be different, when they became concrete and real, not the abstract sense of a bulging belly and regular movements, but an individual made of squishy flesh and a being who existed separate from me.

Further advice he gave was to talk to a neonatologist at our local hospital as soon as we could to discuss the range of care available and to make sure we were on the same page. Was our desire to have this baby live as long as medically possible, or to provide as pain-free an exit as we could?

He also asked if we had a children's hospice in our area and suggested calling soon to register with them and to understand the variety of services they offered.

'Do send me through your birth plans, once you've written them, if you'd like me to have a look over them, and get in touch if you think of any more questions.' He ended the conversation as kindly and supportively as he'd started, even though he couldn't offer us any reassurance that things were going to play out any differently.

'Thank you. Thank you for talking with us today and for all your advice.' While we appreciated him taking the time to talk to us, we ended the Zoom call shell-shocked and horrified.

'What did he say?' My mother was keen to hear good news, but we had none to offer. I felt so heavy, sorrow weighing down my features and communicating our agony.

The inevitability of our baby's suffering and death was now inescapably in front of us. I had looked to him for hope as a drowning person clutches at long grass near the edge of a lake, and found no hand hold, no buoyancy aid, just a handful of useless strands sinking with me.

14
Calling the hospice

2nd December 2021 (continued)

That afternoon, when I was alone in the house, I took the neonatologist's advice and called the hospice.

I had to explain why I was calling in order to be put through to the right department, and explaining the situation we were in made it feel all too real. I was soon talking to a community nurse, Eve.

'First of all, congratulations on your pregnancy,' she said, which caught me off guard and caused my heart to swell.

'Thank you,' I replied, amazed at how affirming it felt to be congratulated and have this pregnancy acknowledged as still a positive thing. It was my first indication of how hospices see the whole person and treat cases as individuals, not as stereotypes. It was a recognition that this baby was precious and wasn't going to be seen or treated as solely a genetic condition. Her opening sentence stayed with me and began a process of building up a sense of worth and care that I desperately wanted but hadn't experienced in the clinical hospital setting.

She communicated such tenderness as we spoke that I felt a deep comfort begin to enfold me, like being wrapped in a thick, soft blanket.

We spent twenty minutes talking as she detailed the incredible variety of what they offered: residential rooms for end-of-life care, with twenty-four-hour nursing provided; family suites for siblings; complimentary meals; memory-making mementos; a large garden and play area outside.

We had been told no family, not even our children, could visit the baby in the hospital, but extended family were welcome in the large garden surrounding the hospice. They could come and visit and so get to meet the baby, hopefully living. Therefore this baby, who was so real to me, could be as real and alive to them and so become a part of the family in their memories as well. I so wanted this baby to be as special to them as to me.

She talked me through the care offered at home, should we wish to take the baby back with us for a day or so after they had passed. We could borrow a cold cot, which keeps the baby's body at a suitable temperature, if we wanted to have the experience of bringing the baby home and having some time in our own house as a family of five. One of the devastating experiences people recall after baby loss is leaving the hospital with no baby; giving birth and leaving with empty arms. Allowing the baby to come home, even for only one night, can prevent that particular memory from forming.

She also explained about the counselling and support they would offer the whole family, for up to three years. While the hospital did kindly offer bereavement counselling, it was limited to three months, which seemed like a good start but hardly a suitable length of time to truly journey with someone deep in grief. Three years felt more accurate in terms of the length of time to start to come to terms with the loss of a child, or at least learning how to live around the loss.

I began to wonder if this experience might not be as harrowing as I'd first feared because, through it all, there would be people alongside us who knew what to do and what to say in exactly the right way. People who would know how to care, not only for me and the baby, but also for Paul and the children, so I could perhaps pause the mental load of caring for them and just focus on this baby for as long as I was able. I might have space to soak in and grieve, without having to also carry the load of the household tasks and keeping the kids occupied.

As I heard all these details and experienced this understanding and kindness, I realised I'd built up defences to deal with the coldness of how I'd been treated at the hospital. In a self-preservation attempt, to some extent I'd turned off accessing the depth of my emotions and had turned on the safety of feeling numb. The nurse's compassionate manner started to melt these defences as I began to envision what my baby's last days might look like in the hospice and how, on some level, it could be survivable because we'd be taken care of and looked after and I wouldn't have to fight for their care. I'd be surrounded by people who saw the baby as a valid person in their own right and deserving of tenderness and protection.

As we drew to the end of the conversation, she explained I'd need to get my midwife to fill in a referral form, and she started to take down my details. We got through name and date of birth and then she paused when I gave the address of where we were living at the time.

'Sorry, let me go and check something,' she said as I waited on the line.

'I am so sorry,' she said on her return. 'I should have checked where you lived at the start the conversation. You mentioned the hospital, which is in our catchment area, and so I assumed you lived in the town too. I am so sorry but you're out of the county and therefore out of our catchment area.'

'No, no, please, God no,' I quietly prayed inside. 'Please don't take this away from me.'

I felt desperate. Undone. It was too late to haul the defences back up and now I could feel the devastation as all the care and compassion was pulled away, not just like a rug from beneath my feet but as if the whole floor had retracted, and now I was falling. It was as if I'd relaxed in the comfort of the warm blanket, and it being quickly yanked off had left me painfully exposed.

'There is a hospice in your county, although it is on the other side from you so not as close as us. I advise you to call them when you're able and I'm sure they'll be able to offer all we've talked through.'

I was too distraught to speak and couldn't hold back the tears. The dam of grief I'd been trying to hold inside broke as I only saw the cold clinical nature of the hospital environment navigating us through our baby's death, as a long drive felt impossible for us with a terminally ill baby and two preschoolers.

She asked if I was OK and I squeaked a response, then said I had to go.

Grateful to be alone, I cried so hard. I cried for the care I'd never get to receive, for the way the news had been broken to us, for the baby I might never get to meet, for the way I'd now have to navigate my own grief as well as my children's without the expertise of the hospice staff, and how this baby might never come home with us, awake or asleep.

When my mother returned with the children, she asked if I'd got through to the hospice, and I nodded.

'They can't take us because we're outside of their catchment area.' My voice cracked and, sensing my anguish, she gave me a hug. But I didn't want a hug. I wanted the kindness, empathy, knowledge and professionalism of the hospice to accompany us on this journey. I wanted the defences back so I didn't have to feel all this pain. More than anything, I wanted to regain the feeling that maybe the misery of this experience might be mitigated because we'd be walked through it all by people who understood and cared and could tell us that what we were feeling was normal, and could remind us this baby was real and cherished and a person of worth in their own right. But it was gone. And the numbness was gone. And all that was left was the expectation of death and grief. I wished I'd never known what they offered and how they cared. I wish I hadn't called and been left bereft. Yet I also wished this baby was healthy and well, and what could I do to make that happen? This new reality felt like trauma upon trauma.

15
Questions

3rd December 2021

I called the new hospice the next day, my feelings dulled and despondent. Once again, I heard the list of what could be offered, but none of it felt relevant because it was so far away.

'I can't imagine we'll bring the baby down your way because of the distance,' I told them. We knew we wanted our children to keep to their familiar routines as much as possible, so we didn't want them staying a long way from preschool and playgroups. One of the draws of the hospice close to the hospital was that they could still attend preschool from there or could stay at home overnight, in their own beds, and visit daily if it didn't work out for them to stay at the hospice with us. Then their lives could continue as normal, albeit with grandparents in attendance rather than us, while we could focus on the little newborn.

'Counselling? Oh yes, we'd definitely access the counselling if we could do it online?' There was only one thing I could see this hospice providing for us and I wasn't going to turn it down.

I also called the hospital back that day. We had no more appointments booked and I didn't know what was going to happen next. I called the screening coordinator as it was the only number I had and she would know who I was without me having to give an explanation.

She informed me nothing would happen for the next two weeks as we wouldn't be able to meet with further members of the team, such as a neonatologist, until we were at a gestation that meant we were likely to need their services. I guessed they didn't want to waste their time in case this baby died too soon, so they wanted to wait until I was further along, when the likelihood of a stillbirth had decreased. I didn't appreciate that very much. It didn't seem fair to wait another few months to know what the options were if my baby were born conscious. Would I need to fight for this baby to receive care? I would have to live with the uncertainty of not knowing until this baby had shown they weren't going to pass away quietly.

I asked what would happen if I stopped feeling movement as, though I'd been told to prepare for a stillbirth, they'd not talked me through who to contact or what would happen.

'Ah yes, you do need to know that now,' she agreed, communicating again her belief this baby was doomed and past help. It seemed getting in touch with my midwife was the first step and then coming in for a scan. 'Best to keep a hospital bag in your car, you know, just in case you need to stay in after the scan and deliver the baby.' I didn't want that reminder in my car, a harbinger of death, prompting anticipatory grief every time I opened the boot. I decided I'd pack that bag when I needed it, and not before.

Neither conversation left me feeling uplifted or reassured. Both contributed to a settling sense of heaviness that I shrugged on like a weighted jacket and which seemed designed to drag me down.

It wasn't only these conversations contributing to the load but also questions circulating around my mind that I had no answers for.

One thing we were having to decide for the following academic year was which infant school to apply to for Martha. We lived behind one that seemed excellent but was large, and in preschool she'd been a shy and quiet child, causing the staff there to question if this school would suit her. Another school, closer to the preschool but further from us, was half the size and had a special unit for children with special educational needs and disabilities. I found myself debating which school would be better for us as a whole family should this baby live.

Would the closer school be a better fit, because perhaps I could find a friend to take Martha to school and pick her up if it was difficult to take the baby out of the house or if we had a lot of medical appointments? Or would the school further away, with its specialised unit, be perfect, because this baby might have a place they could attend and thrive? I just didn't know.

There was also a deeper question rumbling around that I was afraid to acknowledge.

Had I, in some way, caused this?

My older two had both been born late in the year, when the nights feel cold and never-ending and the long feeds, or attempted feeds, are not aided by the layers of clothing needed to keep warm. I had decided, for our third, I would aim for a spring baby as I wanted to experience the shorter nights and warmer temperatures for those initial difficult weeks of establishing breastfeeding and trying to keep a small baby warm. It sounds silly to write all of this out, as if it was a fully thought through and conscious choice when, in reality, these things can rarely be planned!

I'd thought we could aim for a May baby and so decided on a date to stop taking contraception. Then I realised it was going to be 2022 and I thought, flippantly, how fun it would be to have a date of birth of 02/2022 so decided to stop taking the pill a few months earlier and see. In the end, our due date was March so I'd missed the February birth date anyway, and now I couldn't shake the question, 'What if I had waited?'

What if I had waited and stuck with the original plan? Would we now have a healthy pregnancy, which I'd be taking for granted, having no clue about genetic conditions and extra chromosomes? Would we have skipped over this whole experience, sidestepping it with complete ignorance of the family trauma we'd missed?

A character in the Bible, originally called Sarai, hearing that God had promised her husband a son and knowing she was infertile, arranged for him to impregnate her slave girl. This was not the plan God had, as Sarai became pregnant and gave birth to a son many years later, and this poor son of the slave woman was rejected and discarded. Sarai is used as an example of not trusting that God can work out His own plans in His own way in His own timing, but acting as if He needs our help. She had a promise but not the trust to let it happen without any interference.[16]

Her story came to mind as I wondered if my interference had caused this. If I had been patient and waited for the timing I'd originally felt, would I have saved myself this heartache? Had my impatience and flippancy of wanting a certain date of birth meant I'd doomed my own child?

I didn't have an answer, and I didn't have the confidence or courage to sit with these questions in prayer and see if God had anything to say to me. Instead, I tried to ignore them, push them to one side and pretend they didn't exist.

---

[16] Genesis 15–18, 21.

16
Stillbirth is still birth

4th December 2021

I once watched an episode of a documentary set in a maternity unit and delivery suite, which followed a foetal medicine consultant who was caring for complex pregnancies. This was when I still lived in a world where I thought most babies were born animate and healthy.

I was not prepared to hear that one of the mothers featured had stopped feeling movement and the baby's heart was no longer beating. The baby in her womb, at thirty-seven weeks gestation, had died.

What happened next was tactfully shown: a labour and birth coloured with the tragic knowledge that this baby was never going to cry or suckle or even move.

The term 'stillbirth' suddenly made devastating sense.

Normally, a birth of a live baby involves crying and lots of movement as they go from the cosy, tight enclosure of the womb into the vast open space outside, and they cry with shock and flail their limbs, looking for the familiar boundary of their mother's tummy.

With a stillbirth, there's no sound. No flailing. Just silence. And stillness.

It was the most tragic thing I had ever seen.

What should have been a joyous and wondrous moment of new life coming into the world was instead desperately sad, void of sound and movement. It felt like a black hole of emotion sucking away all that feels good and right and leaving a terrible sense of injustice and desolation. This innocent, unique life should have had a chance, a go, at life!

But no. The mother cradled the baby to her chest as silent tears slipped down her cheeks and the midwife had to leave the room to hide her own distress. This baby was loved and precious and... absent.

When I watched this episode and encountered this deep grief, I had no idea that in a few years' time, this would be the very experience I would be expecting to face.

I absolutely took it for granted that my pregnancies were healthy and my babies born moving and well. My arrogance and naivety were now laid to rest.

I wrote a birth plan for a stillbirth while staying at my parents' house, communicating my desire for the birth to be as similar to my previous two as possible, with low lighting and soft music to create a calm and peaceful environment. I wanted the announcement of the gender to be a positive moment, more like celebrating whether a boy or girl were joining our family than commiseration for the son or daughter we were losing. I requested that the baby be laid on my chest and for us to be left as long as we needed. I wanted to cuddle and rock and sing to my baby, capturing and condensing all the lost long nights of being desperate for the baby to fall asleep, instead of being desperate for this baby to wake up.

I asked for us to be able to bath and dress the baby and have time to take photos together. I wanted the pastor of our church to be able to come and pray for us all together, perhaps the one time we'd be physically complete as a family of five on this earth. I requested hand and footprints to be taken so we could treasure these physical mementos and proof that our baby had existed, even if they would never leave smudged fingerprints all over our windows and even if their feet never left marks in the snow or trailed mud and sand into the car and round our house.

I didn't want to leave the hospital with an empty car seat, so added that we would like to take the baby to the hospice ourselves. I did not want to mar the memories of my previous joyful births with the final, potentially traumatic and life-changing one. I wanted to know love and comfort would be there, even in the midst of the shadow of death.

I wanted to pray over the baby and worship God, even in the darkest place of my grief.

I know God doesn't promise an easy life or a life without difficulty; as Philippians 3 points out, if we're following Jesus then we share in His sufferings, but that passage also promises that we will 'know the power of his resurrection' (Philippians 3:10). God does promise to always be with us with a refrain that echoes through the Bible: 'he will never leave you nor forsake you' (Deuteronomy 31:8; see also Hebrews 13:5). Jesus promises His followers, 'And surely I am with you always, to the very end of the age' (Matthew 28:20) and says the Holy Spirit will 'help you and be with you for ever' (John 14:16). I knew I could rely on His comfort and presence remaining with me.

So I contemplated my own worst nightmare and saw I would not be crushed by the darkness because the source and creator of all light would always be there, even in the 'valley of the shadow of death' (Psalm 23:4, NKJV). At the same time, I desperately clung on to hope that this was somehow all wrong and this vibrant and active baby inside me would not one day go still forever.

17
Naming

8th-12th December 2021

We returned home from our early Christmas at my parents' place to a cold house and a vase full of flowers. Our next-door neighbour had rescued two deliveries of flowers from our front step, arranged them and put them in water so our kind friends' gifts wouldn't be wasted and to save us returning to two dried-up bouquets of dead buds on our doorstep.

Friends from out of town came to visit the next day, easing me back into being the sole childcare provider after a week of help and providing much appreciated presence. It always seems to be harder to be alone with kids after having lots of help because you relax and get used to not carrying all the load of housework and behaviour management. You can share out their desire for attention and every single question they feel compelled to ask! Add in pregnancy's load on the body and disturbed sleep, and it can be challenging to remain patient and calm in the face of all their needs. Also, I found having other adults around provided distraction, drawing me out of dark thoughts and helping to keep me rooted in the present.

I had been due to meet with a group of friends in the evening, but one messaged to say her son had been sent home from nursery with a temperature. Four members of his class had already tested positive for Covid and so I cancelled. It wasn't a fear of getting the virus itself, but what would happen if I did. Isolating for ten days would mean missing our next appointment and I couldn't take the risk of missing any potential deterioration in our baby's condition.

The next morning was my son's taster session at preschool and after the hour was up, we walked all the way home: a fifteen-minute walk taking an hour as he stopped to fill the pram with stones and pick leaves and winter berries on the way.

Lunchtime ended up being full of phone calls as he napped: the bereavement midwife from the hospital called to make contact, and a specialist nurse called Sarah arranged to meet us before our next scan to have a tour of 'skiboo' and the Forget-Me-Not suite in the maternity unit. I had to ask Paul what 'skiboo' might be and he laughed as he explained it was 'SCBU' or the Special Care Baby Unit.

'Hospital talk.' He rolled his eyes. 'Hospital staff sometimes forget there's a world outside and that uninitiated people have no idea what they're talking about. Doctors who work in A&E refer to it as the "shop floor", which I never got on with.'

The next phone call came later that afternoon as we walked back from picking up Martha, and it was the community nurse from the hospice, Eve.

'I wanted to make sure you're receiving the care you'd like from the other hospice? You've been on my mind all week and I wanted to check in with you.'

'Thank you,' I replied. 'That's kind of you. I did speak with them last week and they have offered us their services. We agreed we'd take them up on counselling but, to be honest, we're not going to take the baby there because it's too far away.'

Then she offered us a lifeline.

'Would you like me to speak on your behalf and argue that you could be an exceptional case with us here? Sometimes it does happen that we can take on cases that aren't in our catchment area. I'm not promising anything! I do feel for you and want to make sure you're receiving the care you need.'

Hope stirred inside as I remembered the desperate prayer I'd uttered in my heart at the end of our last phone call.

'Yes, please do. That would be fantastic. I do understand it's not a given, and I appreciate you calling back to check and even offering this. It would make a difference to have somewhere close by to take the baby and have our children visit. To be honest, even knowing we have that in place would make a difference mentally as we anticipate what this whole thing might look like.'

After she rung off, I prayed again, expressing my desire for this hospice care to be offered to us and also acknowledging God knows the end from the beginning, and He knew if we would need it or not, and so I entrusted it all into His hands.

Eve called back in the morning to say the hospice had agreed to take us on as an exceptional case and they would liaise with the medical professionals at the hospital to provide the care and support we needed.

It was incredible news. Something lost or stolen and then recovered can be more precious than something always owned.

'I think this will make all the difference,' I remember telling Paul. I was so grateful I didn't have to steel myself against the harsh clinical nature of hospital existence while potentially watching my delicate little baby being treated as a medical issue. Instead, I could relax and breathe, knowing we'd be supported every step of the way and knowing our baby would be in the hands of expert, compassionate nurses who also knew how to carry us through this impending dark time.

'The hospice has agreed to take us on as an exceptional case,' I was enormously pleased to tell my family, and also witness their relief at knowing we'd be taken care of in a way they wouldn't be able to offer.

It was good news for us all.

We had been discussing and deciding the name of our baby, while the gender remained a mystery.

For a boy, we had decided to carry over Daniel, which had been Jamie's original middle name, until he'd been born and it was exchanged in a burst of paternal pride for his father's name. We added David as a middle name in homage to Paul's twin brother.

Daniel in the lions' den and David and Goliath are well known children's Sunday school stories. Daniel stood firm by his faith and rhythm of praying three times a day even when commanded not to, and so was punished by being put into a den with lions to be eaten alive. We are told God 'shut the mouths of the lions' (Daniel 6:22) and he was spared, much to the surprise and joy of the king who'd been tricked into condemning him but had respect and affection for him.[17]

David was a shepherd boy who, offended at his nation's God being ridiculed by the champion of their enemy's army, a giant named Goliath, offered to challenge him single-handed. Using a slingshot and stones he collected from a stream, trusting God would not let His name be maligned, he killed Goliath with a single shot to the forehead.[18]

Both of these biblical figures should have died. Both lived. Their trust in God and how they stood firm in challenging times set an example for us.

So the baby was to be Daniel David if it was a boy.

For a girl, I'd settled on Rachel Elizabeth, solely because I think it's a pretty name.

Until one night when I kept waking up, not just stirring and returning to sleep but feeling wide awake, as if to start the day. I found myself thinking about the name we'd chosen and how something about it wasn't fitting. I have a lovely, kind and generous aunt called Rachel and a fantastic close friend with the name who lived nearby. I couldn't name a baby who was going to die after them. It didn't feel right.

During one of the episodes of dozing between the wakeful periods, I dreamed this baby was a girl and the name seemed so obvious that it couldn't be anything else. This name felt as fitting as an apple being called an apple. The name was Hope.

Hope defined our response to the diagnosis and our journey. You can't keep hope down. No matter how battered I would feel after a scan or conversation with a medical person about

[17] Daniel 6.
[18] 1 Samuel 17.

how this might all play out, hope would always break through again like desert flowers appearing after a sudden rainfall. I couldn't not hope. It was irresistible. Over and over again in my diary, I wrote about my hope that this baby would live. After this particulate night, I wrote, 'We will always have hope this baby will live and experience joy and know our love.'

And so, she became Hope, and would always define for us the value of holding on to hope, even when it feels that is all you've got.

18
Every Life Counts

13th-15th December 2021

A charity in Ireland called Every Life Counts supports parents who've been given a life-limiting diagnosis for their child. I'd been told about it by a mother of a little girl called Jovie who was born with a severe brain condition called holoprosencephaly.[19] Even though the doctors thought she might not live, Jovie was nine months old and absolutely adored by her parents and siblings. Her mother, Deborah, had been supported by Vicky from Every Life Counts and suggested I get in touch.

While Jamie had his first morning without me at preschool, I had a long conversation with Vicky over the phone. She was so positive and kind, having lost her own baby Líadán in 2014. Líadán had been born sleeping at thirty-two weeks after being diagnosed with Trisomy 18 during the pregnancy. She had been encouraged to 'pop over to England' for a termination as they weren't available in Ireland at the time, and was a wealth of knowledge, experience and encouragement for me.

'How are you feeling?' she asked me.

'To be honest…' I paused to consider. 'Hopeful. If I'm being perfectly honest.'

'That's great. Listen, it definitely is a good thing that they can't see anything wrong with your baby's heart. That is a very good sign. Those babies tend to live longer.

---

[19] www.joviesjourney.org.uk (accessed 13th November 2024).

'These doctors are always so pessimistic and bleak, don't you listen to them!' she continued. 'They always prepare you for the worst. Listen, make sure you're also prepared to bring the baby home with you. We've had some babies who fared far better than expected and the parents were totally unprepared! Make sure you've got things in place for if the baby does come home from the hospital.'

I could feel hope rising as she spoke. She'd journeyed with so many families over the years and probably had more experience of the range of outcomes than the doctors who signposted termination and then had little to do with the postnatal period of any of the babies born alive.

'Now, we offer a few different things to help at this time. We pack memory boxes for the baby which we send in the post; they contain tiny baby clothes, books and wee little teddies – mementoes for you to photograph the baby with and then keep. Each one is uniquely constructed, for each family, and I can post it to you, even in the UK.'

I'd heard of this kind of thing before and it seemed so sweet and special.

'That would be lovely, thank you.'

'And we provide support with writing birth plans. I can email you some birth plan templates which you're free to use, and then also some other families' birth plans for you to look at for reference, and then we'd ask you to delete them, out of respect and privacy for the family.'

'Oh yes, thank you. I have been told I need to write a birth plan and that would be helpful.'

Vicky would check in with me regularly over the coming weeks and call periodically to see how things were going and how I was coping. That level of support was incredible, knowing I had someone I could call to offload emotionally or ask any questions; someone who I'd already spoken to and knew my situation so I didn't have to repeat myself or explain again; someone who got what I was going through because they'd already been there themselves.

Her encouragement to prepare for bringing the baby home stirred up thoughts about what it might look like if that happened. One of my cousins was born with a genetic condition and although, as a child, I didn't see the full extent of what caring for him meant to my aunt and uncle, I got a glimpse. I was aware of the vast challenges and difficulties of having a child with disabilities, and wondered what the impact on my family of four would be. I imagined multiple hospital stays and the stress that would place on having two kids at home to look after and a husband working full-time. I wondered whether the older two would resent having a lot less attention and struggle behaviourally when they felt ignored or neglected due to their younger sibling's needs.

Even though caring for young children and ageing parents is an intrinsic part of being family, both of those are normally limited to a period of time, a span of years at most, and come to an end as children grow more independent and parents pass away. Caring for a child with complex medical needs who will never be able to look after themselves calls for a deeper sacrifice and laying down of your life than most people ever have to face. I wondered if this meant I'd never return to work, as I'd become a full-time carer, and how my current activities would have to change.

That night, Paul and I sat watching television as I shared with him my conversation with Vicky.

'Quick!' I grabbed Paul's hand. 'Feel here, you might be able to feel the baby move!'

I'd been feeling the baby's movements for months already, but it hadn't been long since the pushes and ripples were perceptible from the outside and not just internally. Any time I'd felt my belly distend or stretch with my hand, I quickly tried to have Paul feel it. So far it hadn't worked and the movements had ceased before he could feel anything.

This evening, however, was different.

'Oh wow,' he said. 'I can feel it!'

Feeling a baby move while inside the womb is a crazy and awesome thing. Seeing a pregnant woman's belly move by itself is astonishing, with the waves of movement and sometimes even a discernible hand or foot.

This experience was meaningful on a whole new level. This was the first time Paul had felt the baby physically, and therefore knew they were alive on an experiential level and not just in theory.

'This is a radically different journey for you, isn't it?' he said softly.

'Yes. Yes, it is.' This baby was not a theoretical concept to me. They were undeniably real.

'You know there's a real-life baby moving inside,' he marvelled.

He was not only coming to terms with how active this baby was, but how this had shaped my bonding and relationship with them for weeks now.

'Yes, I feel the movement multiple times a day.'

We were bonded in such a way that no one could tell me this baby didn't have value in their own right, and I would do all I possibly could to give them not only a chance at life, but one filled with love and affection. I was a lioness, ready to fight tooth and claw against any predator who threatened my precious cub.

19
Another scan, another opinion

16th December 2021

Our next scan loomed.

I anticipated appointments with a real mixture of emotion. They were the only way we had of finding out if the baby was doing OK, so I craved seeing the little heartbeat on the screen and knowing for sure they were still with us. I desired to have as much information as possible, without any invasive tests, so we could prepare appropriately. At the same time, I dreaded them. I dreaded being in the powerless position of having a medical figure listing things they'd found wrong with my baby when I couldn't interpret the information on the screen and therefore verify what was being said. I didn't have any evidence that this baby wasn't perfectly healthy other than their words and one blood test. The anticipation was high as I wondered what would be found this time – as the baby grew bigger, it'd be easier to see on scans if there were any abnormalities in their heart or brain. I steeled myself for bad news, pessimism and a crushing of hope once again.

We'd arranged to meet Sarah, the specialist nurse, in SCBU half an hour before the scan, for a quick tour. We weren't able to enter the wards, only walk down the hallway, and then we chatted with her in the family room. She agreed that attitudes towards genetic conditions have changed in the medical world, although she did still reiterate the likelihood of our baby passing and the need for us to prepare for that. She explained how the unit worked and how, if the baby did spend any time there, I could stay with them on the ward overnight. She advised us to make decisions on the mode and timing of delivery and explained which interventions could be offered after birth. She also showed us the Forget-Me-Not suite, which is tucked inside the door of the delivery suite in the hospital but feels private. Its purpose is to provide space for a mother delivering a baby who's already died or is expected to die. It is close enough to the rest of the delivery suite to be able to provide adequate staffing and care, but is removed so as to silence the voices of newborn babies and labouring women. I hoped deep down I would never have to use it.

By our allocated appointment time, we were sat in the waiting room of the antenatal screening clinic.

We waited. And waited.

During the waiting time, I started to write up a series of messages friends had sent me after the day of fasting for the baby. They were so encouraging.

An hour and ten minutes later, Dr Richards called us in. Paul made it clear as we entered the room that he hadn't appreciated the wait and might have to leave early to get to his work shift on time. After that, I always made sure I'd brought a book to read in the waiting room and she was never late again!

'Since I last saw you, you've had a positive NIPT test for Trisomy 18 and you saw my colleague soon after that, is that right?'

'Yes,' I replied, 'and they gave our baby an extremely poor prognosis. In fact, they weren't very hopeful at all and it seemed they wanted to make sure we weren't expecting this baby to live.'

'OK,' she mused. 'Have a lie-down here and I'll take a look to see how the baby's doing.'

She chatted away during the scan, explaining things and wondering out loud.

'Looks like the baby's doing well: the growth is on track and it looks to me like the amniotic fluid isn't low at all. Actually, if you don't take the long bones into consideration but use the head and tummy measurements, then the baby would be on the tenth percentile, which would give us no cause for concern. To be honest, I see no markers for Trisomy 18 at all, other than the growth restriction.'

She was being so positive, we started to feel confused. Was she saying there wasn't anything wrong with this baby, or was she just trying to be upbeat to counteract the negative experience we'd had before?

'This just looks like a small baby to me,' she affirmed, and hope rose again. 'If you're sure you don't want an amniocentesis now, when the risk of premature rupture of membranes is higher, we could schedule one for thirty-six weeks? Then there wouldn't really be any risk to the baby as it'd be safe to give birth, and it'd tell us what we're dealing with so we can more accurately plan for the delivery. If the baby does have the condition, then you might decide that a planned Caesarean gives the baby the best chance of surviving birth, but if it doesn't, then you might prefer to have an induction? The baby could have another condition or something else causing the growth restriction and it would be best to know for sure what's going on.'

Part of me was so eager to know for certain what ailed our baby that I did wonder on and off over the coming weeks if we should have taken up the offer of an amnio. I felt acutely that we couldn't take any risks, so we decided to see if we could live with the uncertainty.

'I'm not saying I think the baby will survive, because it is so small,' she continued, 'but the option remains to seek another opinion and be seen in a specialist hospital?'

We came away a bit dazed. *So there is a chance the baby might not have the condition, but there is a chance it might have something else – so are we still preparing to have a baby who dies, or are we not? What happened to the amniotic fluid? Had it been low before or not? Was it suddenly fine or were different consultants seeing different things?* Paul and I discussed our confusion.

'She said we could see a specialist in the other hospital, so maybe we should do that? They might have more experience of babies with different conditions and so they might be able to tell us if ours has it or not?' That felt like the closest thing to certainty we could attain, without potentially causing our baby any harm. It seemed like a good plan and so we agreed to pursue that course of action.

20
Yorkshire Christmas

24th-29th December 2021

Unfortunately, Paul had to work on Christmas Eve and so we planned to drive up to his parents' house as soon as he was finished. I spent the morning packing, keeping an eye on the children and moving them between floors as I needed to shift location.

Our car was in the garage, being fixed, and we'd been offered the use of a loan car over the festive period, although the boot space was about half the size of our own spacious family saloon. Some careful planning needed to be done on what would be left behind, and we settled on the Christmas presents! We didn't have presents for each other as, sadly, our booking of a theatre trip was cancelled due to Covid striking the cast, and the kids would receive presents from family up north so we decided they could have a prolonged Christmas of opening more presents once we were home again.

Paul managed to get away from work early and we were on the road by mid-afternoon. I kept Martha and Jamie entertained for the first half of the journey with books, games and snacks, then we stopped at a service station halfway for tea and to change them into pyjamas. Back in the car for the next part of the journey, they fell asleep in their car seats soon after their normal bedtime. We felt like we were winning.

We arrived at 9pm and quickly transferred a sleeping Jamie into his travel cot, but Martha woke up and sat with Nanna watching *Cinderella* as we sorted out her monitor and sleeping bag. This turned out to be a bad move, as she then took a long time to settle and woke multiple times in the night to ask questions (Why had the stepmother been so cruel? Why had the pumpkin become a carriage?), which was exhausting.

As we eventually settled into our bed, warm and snug, knowing we'd arrived for Christmas and now was the time to relax and enjoy, I suddenly became aware I'd not felt the baby move all day. It was a sickening realisation. I had been so busy packing and entertaining the children in the car, and then with the bustle of arriving… maybe I'd just not noticed?

My mind ran on ahead to what would I do if I didn't feel any movement tomorrow, on Christmas Day? I couldn't tell anyone, that I knew for sure, because I didn't want to ruin the day or for anyone to have future Christmases tarnished by the memory of rushing me to hospital only to discover there was no heartbeat. I didn't know what to do – should I call my midwife and head back home to deliver in our local hospital, or should I go to the hospital here and ask for a scan, explaining the situation we were in? How long after discovering a baby has died in the womb does one deliver? I didn't know. I did know I didn't want to give birth up here, so would we be cutting our holiday short to head back home for a stillbirth? I decided all of this could wait until Boxing Day and I'd handle Christmas Day first, hoping the busyness and fun of the day could keep my mind off things.

Jamie woke up before 6am, which didn't feel the kindest way to start Christmas, but he was all cuddles and cuteness so it was easy to forgive. The house was bustling with lunch preparations going on and Paul's older sister and her three children visiting. The children opened the presents from family and we video-called my parents so they could watch the frantic unwrapping and desire to unpack everything and play with it all immediately. Soon it was time for church and so we bundled up in thick coats and hats and gloves and walked there, enjoying the quiet of the town on Christmas morning.

Paul's parents' church has a lovely community feel, and many people greeted us as we entered and commented on how big the kids were getting. We sang a few hymns, the children all went to the front to show off their toys and then Paul's mother took them out to the creche when the sermon started. The preacher spoke about the hope we have in Christ coming to earth, and how we now don't need to pay the punishment for our own sins because He took it for us in His death on the cross.

All of a sudden, the baby moved. Not just weak or slight movement, but this baby was going for it! Strong, unambiguous actions, signalling to me this baby was not only alive, but full of strength and energy. I laid my hands across my belly to feel the ripples and stretching on the outside too, trying to hammer home that this baby was in no way dead but full of vigour! Tears silently slid down my face as I thanked God for the best Christmas present I could ever have received: the knowledge that, right now, this baby was living and well. There would be no cancelled Christmas this year, and no trip to the hospital with the impending fear of a silent scan.

The rest of the day was joyous as we feasted and were joined by more family, and I was glad I'd not worried anyone or made a big deal out of missing movement because I was too busy to notice.

Our festive period continued with walks and resting and family time and home-cooked food.

I started reading a few books that I'd received for Christmas: *Saying Goodbye* by Zoë Clark-Coates,[20] chronicling her story of coping with multiple baby losses, and *Perfectly Human: Nine Months with Cerian*[21] by Sarah Williams. Her third daughter, Cerian, was diagnosed with skeletal dysplasia at the twenty-week scan and they were told it was fatal. I deeply appreciated reading her story of how she coped with it, how her faith carried her and all she felt God speak to her during the pregnancy and loss.

Even hearing how her colleagues had no idea how to talk to her after her loss was eye-opening, revealing how we as a culture

[20] Zoë Clark-Coates, *Saying Goodbye,* Colorado Springs, CO: David C Cook, 2017.
[21] Sarah C. Williams, *Perfectly Human: Nine Months with Cerian*, New York: Plough Publishing House, 2018.

shy away from difficult or upsetting topics and think we can pretend something hasn't happened. It reminded me how important it is to acknowledge and express sadness and sympathy in a loss, rather than find the awkwardness too much and shy away from saying anything at all.

Dr Clea Harmer, the chief executive of Sands (Stillbirth and Neonatal Death Charity) writes, 'Bereaved parents often feel invisible and alone in their grief … The isolation that parents feel speaks volumes about how society feels unable to talk, or even think, about the tragedy of a baby dying – quite literally struggling to find the words.'[22] An adult who dies often has a wide network of friends, colleagues and family, so people stand together in grief, sharing their sad loss. An unborn baby might not feel real except to its parents and especially the mother, and so no one else can experience the absence they do.

The author faced her own medical crises during the pregnancy, and it prompted me to think of how to gather a community who'd be ready to pray for us should an emergency occur. As the year came to an end, I set up a WhatsApp group for prayer updates for the pregnancy and baby, and within the first evening, ninety of our friends had joined. I felt deeply grateful and greatly supported, knowing this baby was cherished by others and we weren't alone.

Sarah Williams' perspective was shaped by something she'd felt God communicate to her: 'Here is a sick and dying child. Will you love this child for me?'[23] It felt like an invitation we might never want to receive but one we would accept.

The author also wrote of how her husband only properly started to grieve after the baby's birth and passing, and it helped me realise that the true depth of grief and what we were facing might not hit Paul until the baby was born. We may be on different trajectories with our processing and reactions, as a baby really only becomes a reality to the dad at the birth.

---

[22] Sands with Susan Clark, *Loving You From* Here, London: Yellow Kite, 2022, ppvii-viii.

[23] Williams, *Perfectly Human*, p19.

A friend from Paul's schooldays popped round and opened up about the grave challenges his family had faced over the last few years, and I felt that we were better prepared to hold the space for his trauma because of our own. Once you've experienced difficulty, you have so much more time and compassion for those who are suffering. It felt like we were meeting him on the same level in our sufferings, rather than expressing patronising sympathy from afar.

As we headed home, I felt grateful for a meaningful and full Christmas. I didn't want to think about whether this would be our only Christmas as a family of five, but tried to hold on to my gratitude that for now, right at this moment, all of my children were living and together.

21
New Year's Eve

30th-31st December 2021

Our first morning home included the next scan with the consultant, and it showed nothing new. The baby was still growing along the right trajectory, even if that line was off the bottom of the growth chart, and we were grateful no new concerns or abnormalities could be seen. She mentioned she couldn't see any fluid around the heart, although she could see something called placental lakes. I didn't know what that meant, but assumed it wasn't too much of an issue if she didn't seem worried about them.

The consultant had been waiting on our go-ahead to make a referral to the specialist hospital, and we made it clear we'd like to be seen there.

'They are hugely experienced and can answer any questions you have,' the consultant reassured us. 'They may suggest you have an amniocentesis to confirm the diagnosis, so think about that and, also, consider asking their advice on a plan of care if the pregnancy progresses.'

As we drove home, Paul and I shared how we'd experienced the same feeling as we watched the baby move on the screen.

'I find it really hard to believe that this baby won't live,' I stated.

'I know. I agree. They're so active and seem so full of life.'

'Maybe we need to be preparing for life with a disabled child rather than a baby that'll die shortly after birth?'

'Maybe every parent with a diagnosis like ours hopes for the best and finds it hard to accept?'

'Maybe this scan with the specialist will give us some answers?'

We could only hope.

As Martha and Jamie played together in the afternoon, I started to pack a hospital bag. After the scare over Christmas, I knew I had to face this. I wanted to be ready when the time came, and not find myself putting together all I'd need for a hospital stay while carrying a baby in my womb who I knew had already passed.

Having had two babies in hospital already, I knew what I needed for myself: all the awkward items nobody talks about like maternity pads and breast pads, as well as loose-fitting, comfy clothes and toiletries. But when it came to packing for the baby, I paused. Normally you pack a few sets of clothes and nappies and wet wipes and a muslin and nappy bags... and I didn't know if I'd need any of these. Would I ever need to change this baby's nappy? Would this baby ever need a second set of clothes? Where would I even get hold of teeny-tiny baby clothes?

Overcome with the torment of these questions, I shut the bag and put it to the side. I didn't need to deal with this right now. I decided this could wait until after the scan, which I hoped would give me a better sense of what we would be expecting.

New Year's Eve started with a phone call directly from the consultant to say she'd written personally to the specialist in the larger hospital to explain our situation, and she'd also referred through the usual means.

'You probably won't hear from them until next week, but you can expect to be given an appointment in the following ten days,' she told me.

At lunchtime I received a phone call from a withheld number.

'Hello, I'm a midwife from the Foetal Medicine Unit and we've received a referral for you. Would you be able to come in at 3.30pm on Tuesday 4th January?'

'Yes! Yes, we can. We can make arrangements. Thank you, that was quick.'

I phoned Paul as soon as our conversation was over to let him know, and to check if he could get the time off work to go. I phoned my parents and they agreed to come up and stay to look after the kids.

Then the nerves set in.

Would this appointment be the big reveal? Would we get any clue whether our baby would be one of the Edwards' babies who survived, or would the initial devastating prognosis be reiterated and confirmed? I also wondered what the specialist's manner would be like and how they'd make us feel. It can make such a difference being told tragic and upsetting news with empathy and compassion.

Here was an opportunity to take deep breaths, remind myself this was all in God's hands and choose not to dwell on the anxious thoughts.

I posted on Instagram to start the year:

What if 2022 is a year of miracles, where a baby lives and a diagnosis is shown to have been a false positive?

Yes, my world changed in 2021.

I now live in a world where babies die & I can no longer take the health & life of my loved ones for granted; where the awful things that happen to other people, have visited my family; where uncertainty is my daily companion, though not fear or anxiety about what is to come. I've navigated enough in my life so far to know the promise of God's presence & provision is real, can be relied upon & always comes through when you need it.

I've come to see we live in a world where there is no limit on suffering, no equal fair sharing of trauma. Some people get it heaped upon heap, while others escape unscathed. There's no reason why. It's just the world we live in.

The hand we've been dealt for 2022 seems fraught with pain, grief, confusion, wondering. I don't deny that. I also sense a deep invitation to meet God in the suffering in a sweet way we would never have known otherwise. You don't need His comfort when you feel happy, healthy & whole. You can't empathise unless you've been down in the pit yourself. My heart might be totally broken this year.

Oh God, may it be broken open to be flooded by your love & compassion, making me into a person who can stand to remain with others in the depths of their despair, without trying to save them from it or lessen their experience due to my discomfort, giving glib answers or comparing to others worse off. May my heart be able to hold the silence as the tears stream, just being a presence with, knowing love sometimes is just staying and saying, 'I'm so sorry.'

I'd love 2022 to be a year where I don't hold a baby as it dies… my baby, my precious, precious love. Oh God, I need you to hold my heart this year. I don't think I'll be able to hold it together without the knowledge that you know the beginning from the end, you have ordained every day of this child's life & they're written in your book already. You love this baby more than I could ever imagine & have entrusted us to be its parents & to love & care for it as long as it lives. This is our privilege.

2022, please be kind.

22
The specialist

4th January 2022

We went into this scan feeling hopeful. Surely it made a difference that our baby didn't have any obvious physical abnormalities and that growth was continuing along the right trajectory?

Paul had gone to work in the morning after both of us had slept badly the night before, feeling restless with our worries. Ironically, I remembered saying to a friend that uncertainty and not knowing is the hardest. After we were told it was T18, I decided not knowing can be much better than knowing, because then you retain the possibility of it all being nothing. So here we were again, back-pedalling furiously to the possibility that this baby could just be small, wondering if we'd be advised to get an amniocentesis to find out for sure and desperately hoping we'd leave the consultation feeling lighter because medicine was on our side.

To save ourselves the stress of driving and the extortionate hospital parking fees for almost-impossible-to-find spaces, we asked for a lift, and our pastor, Matt, kindly drove us there and back.

For some reason, I had high expectations of what this hospital would look like. My subconscious clearly associated a greater level of expertise in foetal medicine with a more modern, light, spacious and well-equipped building. I was surprised to be faced with a dated, sprawling structure that looked cramped, crowded and slightly run down inside. My memory might be painting a dingy scene of deprivation as a backdrop of the horror to come, rather than correctly recalling the actual scene that day. Either way, there was a jarring contrast to what I had been expecting in the setting, as well as in the scene that played out.

We found the foetal medicine department, filled in a form and were guided to an old sofa in the hallway to wait. We were called in fairly quickly and introduced to two members of staff, but no specialist. I can't remember now if the staff explained what would happen – other memories have superseded and blanked out seemingly insignificant ones.

What did happen was that I was invited to lie on the scanning chair and a member of the team started the scan. I also have no memory of any small talk or if I had to answer any questions about our diagnosis. I do remember explaining we didn't know the gender and would prefer not to find out. I think the sonographer took various measurements of the baby's bones and brain and other organs, and I assumed she was doing some prep work so the specialist could sweep in and give us the interpretation and explanation.

The specialist didn't quite sweep in, but they did make an entrance: they had an entourage following, whose identities I did not keep track of after introductions. Also, I was unable to stand up and greet them face to face, as I still lying prone with my belly exposed, which I found slightly demeaning. I don't think it was intentional or a conscious choice, but our moment of greeting set the stage for the power dynamic that I felt played out. The specialist did put both hands on my shoulders to give a little squeeze as they walked past, which communicated a sense of warmth and connection. This juxtaposition of a warm manner with condescending words would continue throughout the consultation, simultaneously engaging and undermining.

It is hard for a non-medical person like me to imagine how draining it must be for a doctor to frequently deliver heartbreaking news and the barriers they must build to remain in the job over time. I was expecting a level of empathy that is difficult to retain in an environment with such high demands and time constraints.

As far as I remember, the consultation took place as follows.

The specialist started off by joking that they'd received a lot of emails about us from our consultant in the local hospital, as they took over the scanning device.

'Right,' the specialist proceeded, 'let's have a look at this baby.' As the specialist took over the scan, they checked my age and commented on how young I was compared to many of the mothers they saw. Thirty-seven didn't feel young to me, but the specialist commented I was definitely young enough to get pregnant again if we wanted another baby.

I nodded silently, feeling incredulous. Suggesting the ability to have another baby completely ignores the desire of the mother to keep the one she has! Imagine saying to a parent of a child going through chemotherapy, 'Oh well, if this one dies, you can always have another one!' It would be too shocking and offensive to countenance. Yet it seems to be OK to suggest that to someone who may lose a baby in utero.

To be honest, I had no idea before my own pregnancies how devastating a miscarriage could be. I wrongly assumed you could somehow shrug it off and start trying again. I had no idea how a positive pregnancy test changes your whole outlook on life and your plans for the future, and how a sudden bleed can change all of that. The child you'd started to imagine and dream of, as you worked out their due date and imagined what they might look like, suddenly disintegrates into nonexistence. You're left with nothing. I can imagine a late-term pregnancy loss must be even harder as you've had more time to bond and dream and plan and more people to tell it's all over. No future children can take the place of the one lost. You want *that* child, not a replacement.

The specialist had moved on to the brain and I was relieved when they couldn't report anything out of the ordinary there. We saw the feet and hands and then the specialist focused on the face.

'Hmm, now look at this,' they continued as they started to look closely. 'Babies with Trisomy 18 can have something called a cleft lip and it doesn't look like your baby does, but if we zoom in here, let me show you something. The palate is normally seen as a full circle, and here we can see most of the circle but it looks like part of it might be missing. See where the white fades out there and it's black? That could be an indication the baby has a cleft palate.'

I took a sharp breath in as I started to realise that this scan wasn't going to be the reassurance we hoped for but perhaps the opposite, a confirmation of the diagnosis of full T18.

It wasn't long before the specialist found something else.

'Looking at the heart, it seems as if there might be another issue.'

Again, they zoomed in further.

'This technology isn't available in the smaller hospitals,' they explained, 'so we're able to pick up on things they wouldn't be able to see. Are you both medical?'

I said I wasn't and so would appreciate things being explained. The specialist detailed to me the difference between the pulmonary arteries, which carry blood from the right side of the heart to the lungs, and the pulmonary veins, which carry the blood, now oxygen rich, back from the lungs to the heart.

'I think we can see an issue here,' they continued, pointing out a clear bulge in one of the arteries, just before it narrowed. 'This looks like something called pulmonary stenosis, where the valve between the right ventricle and the artery has become narrowed and so the blood can't flow as freely as it ought. It's like a bottleneck: the bulge there is where the blood that should be flowing freely gets stuck and you can see the narrowing here.'

It was clear on the screen, the narrowing and the bulge in the artery, and suddenly, my baby who was going to be one of the fighters, one of the survivors because of a lack of any heart issue, now had one.

'I would expect there to be a discernible murmur on the baby's heart when it's born, and there is no way we could predict how long it would be before this became an issue for their health. It can be operated on, but surgeons might be reluctant for a baby with T18.'

I could feel my energy draining away as we now sat with these two clear structural defects that proved the diagnosis and shortened our expectation of our baby's life. Once again, the emerging sapling of hope had been stamped on, crushed and obliterated as we felt powerless and speechless in a consulting room.

After the specialist finished scanning, they cleaned the jelly off my belly, which normally you're left to do by yourself, and I wondered if they did that as a conscious act of kindness. I sat on a chair next to Paul, on the other side of the table where I'd been lying, and the conversation continued in earnest. The specialist drew down the mask from over their mouth and nose so we could see their face and expressions, which I appreciated.

'You've got the diagnosis and you've seen two consultants. Why have you come to see a third?' they questioned us. I felt wrong-footed by the hostile nature of the question, after their manner had communicated connection and warmth.

'Well,' I mumbled. 'The two seemed to disagree over the severity of what we were dealing with and we've not had an amniocentesis so we don't know for sure, and we were hoping that not having any large structural defects might indicate that our baby might live for longer…' I stumbled on.

'Well, with the positive result on the NIPT test, the small size of the baby and the abnormalities we've seen today, I think we can be pretty confident in saying it's likely we're looking at full Trisomy 18. And actually, an absence of large structural defects isn't a clear indicator of life expectancy. What you've got to understand is that, with genetic conditions like this one, the baby's bodily systems don't work correctly. The enzymes and the hormones and the immune system – they're all compromised and don't function as they should, and this will have a big impact on their health and the length of time they live.'

As the specialist spoke, I felt the heaviness intensify, but also a deep calm. At least now we knew what we were dealing with and the uncertainty was gone. We could prepare.

'The chances of intrauterine demise decrease the longer the pregnancy progresses, so I think would be less than 20 per cent at this stage, but do remember that all babies with full Edwards' die within the first few weeks of life and only about 10 per cent of those with the mosaic form live up to a year.'

As I heard this, I knew the specialist was wrong on the numbers of those born alive, as I'd done so much research and reading. Old studies had shown babies with *full* Edwards' often do die within the first few weeks, but 10 per cent live up to a year – not those with mosaicism. And on top of that, you can't make predictions about babies with the mosaic form as some have so many cells affected that they present as if they have full Edwards' and some have so few that they live a full and healthy life with no clear disabilities.

Did I speak up and challenge the incorrect information they'd given me? No. Do I regret that? Yes.

When they'd finished explaining about the condition, the specialist asked if we had come with any specific questions for them. Now I look back, I wonder why they never mentioned and counselled doing an amniocentesis as we'd expected, but I guess it was a sign of their confidence in the NIPT test and what they'd seen on the scan that they didn't feel it was necessary.

'Yes,' Paul spoke up. 'We know we need to decide on the method and timing of the baby's delivery, and we wondered if you'd have any thoughts on that. We would like to meet the baby alive, and so have assumed that a C-section would be the best option, even though Beth's given birth naturally before.'

'Yes,' the specialist agreed. 'I think natural labour and birth would almost certainly harm the baby, as their body would not be able to survive the stress placed on it. So if your hearts are set on meeting the baby alive, then I would suggest a C-section – although, of course, you do have to take into consideration your other children.'

They then questioned how I'd be able to look after the other children after a C-section and I felt incensed. Even though the neonatologist had prepared us for this kind of pushback, I still found it offensive. How dare someone who had never met my children question my ability to know what was best for us all as a family? I wish I'd had the wherewithal to reply they would be well taken care of by family and friends. Unfortunately, I didn't respond with eloquence but fumbled a defence.

It was another moment that felt like I was blindsided by the difference between the content and the delivery of the specialist's speech. Their manner was warm and comforting but their words cut deep.

'It is harder to advise you on timing, though,' the specialist continued. 'While I would advise regular monitoring, once you've reached thirty-six weeks, that won't always pick things up. The normal methods for checking a baby don't apply here. You could go in for a scan one day and the heart is beating, but return the next and it's not.'

The specialist's words were chilling because this was exactly what had happened to a friend, Helen, I'd made through the SOFT UK Zoom calls. This was also her third pregnancy, but she was further along than me and had had an amniocentesis so knew for sure it was the full genetic condition. She'd shared on the charity's Facebook page about how she'd gone in for a scan with reduced movements on New Year's Eve and been reassured the baby seemed fine and there was a heartbeat. Feeling no movement the next day, she returned and now there was silence. It was utterly heartbreaking.

She returned to the hospital to be induced and had given birth to her beautiful daughter Catherine, or Kitty, on 3rd January. She shared photos of them as a family together with her. The reality felt too close to home and I noted she had been thirty-eight weeks pregnant by this point, and I took it as guidance to deliver the baby by the end of thirty-seven weeks.

My diary entry for that day was mostly about Helen and Kitty, rather than the scan with the specialist. Looking back now, I find that fact surprising because the scan loomed so large and terrifying in my memory. Perhaps I was too distressed to put it into words, knowing capturing it in ink would have made it too real and lasting.

That scan was a turning point for us where we ceased hoping that it all could have been a mistake and began to prepare in earnest for what we'd hoped we'd never have to face. Paul decided he needed to discuss with his work about compassionate leave, to be fully present the whole time the baby might be with us.

The drive home was sombre. It hadn't gone the way we'd wanted and I felt I'd not spoken up when and how I should have. The desire to protect your children is so strong, and I felt I'd not had the position of respect in the room or the courage to overcome that to speak truthfully or confrontationally.

I had a feeling the other people in that room looked at us with pity, not only because we were expecting a baby with a terminal condition, but also because we struggled to accept that reality. That left an unpleasant aftertaste as well, and they would never know what the outcome would be.

The specialist's advice on the need for regular monitoring towards the end, though, would have huge repercussions. I will always be grateful for that advice, although that is skipping ahead a number of weeks.

I ended my diary entry for that day with a decision we'd made: 'Elective C-section last week of February and move to hospice as soon as possible.'

23
Early January

Meeting the specialist completely changed our outlook and now the weeks until the birth became a waiting game. Not a game but a trial – a test of endurance. Every day, I was grateful and relieved to feel movement, and every day we wondered how long we would have to enjoy this baby after birth.

I continued turning to sleep as an escape mechanism as it was the only time I could switch off the nightmare of what we were going through and disappear into a void. Sleep didn't come easily at night, as is common in both pregnancy and grief, and so I napped whenever I could, while both children were at preschool or snatching an hour on the weekend when Paul was home. Night-time seemed to be the only time to process and allow the thoughts I'd pushed to one side during the busyness of the day to squeeze out of their restraints and parade through my mind. It seemed cruel to be kept from sleep overnight – from the ability to block out reality for a few hours, at the only time the children were asleep and I could rest without having the responsibility of looking after them. It also felt unfair, as being more rested enabled me to be a kinder and more patient parent and to experience less physical soreness from the strain of carrying a baby. With each pregnancy, my body seemed to struggle more and more – is it ageing or does the body never fully recover from growing and hauling around a fully grown baby?

A friend suggested I might find comfort and relief in reading the Psalms, a collection of sacred songs and poems in the heart of the Bible. They're honest and raw and passionate, not shying away from troublesome feelings but pouring it all out in prayer. So, starting on the first day of the year, I took her suggestion and read through a psalm a day, and most days wrote a verse down in my diary. It was astonishing and deeply comforting to come across verses that spoke directly to my situation, like, 'The LORD has heard my plea for help; the LORD accepts my prayer … you hold my future … I will bless the LORD who counsels me – even at night when my thoughts trouble me' (Psalm 6:9; 16:5b,7, CSB). Some seemed too good to be true, like, 'the hope of the afflicted will never perish' (Psalm 9:18).

I could scarcely believe that my Hope (if she were a girl) would never perish, but maybe it could mean her story and legacy would live on and have an impact. I wrote in my diary, a week into the new year, 'Her name, Hope, will matter.'

Another baby in the SOFT UK community was born and died after a few hours. My heart broke for them, while also desperately hoping that wouldn't be our story. We heard of another family who were expecting non-identical twins: the boy had T18 and the girl didn't. It was so tricky to know if his health or possible death would affect her being born at full term, and the parents were desolate.

I spoke with the nurse at the hospice about arranging a visit and to discuss who would attend our next big meeting at the hospital, the multi-disciplinary team meeting (MDT). The MDT was to discuss the birth plan and agree on interventions for the baby afterwards. I mentioned that it hadn't felt right looking into funeral arrangements, but that I also didn't want to be doing it in the freshness of bereavement, and she reassured me the hospice could make all the arrangements and we didn't need to be thinking about that now.

Every midwife appointment allowed us to hear a strong, regular heartbeat, and the baby's movements were so vigorous that I struggled to believe death was coming. This baby was vibrant and we were hoping and praying for life, so making plans for death didn't seem fitting. That could come in its own time.

More verses from the Psalms brought encouragement:

> You have granted him his heart's desire
> and have not withheld the request of his lips ...
> He asked you for life, and you gave it to him ...
> (Psalm 21:2,4a)

> It was you who brought me out of the womb,
> making me secure at my mother's breast.
> I was given over to you at birth;
> you have been my God from my mother's womb.
> (Psalm 22:9-10, CSB)

> I remain confident of this:
> I will see the goodness of the LORD
> in the land of the living.
> Wait for the LORD;
> be strong and take heart
> and wait for the LORD.
> (Psalm 27:13-14)

One Sunday, halfway through January, the overall leader of our family of churches, Pete Greig, spoke on Psalm 84 after completing a pilgrimage. As he spoke on the central verses of the psalm, on how God can transform a valley of tears into a place of springs, I read through the rest and found myself deeply touched.

> Even the sparrow has found a home,
> and the swallow a nest for herself,
> where she may have her young –
> a place near your altar,
> LORD Almighty, my King and my God.
> (Psalm 84:3)

I wrote in my diary that evening:

> A home is a place of belonging, of being known, a place
> where you are accepted and loved with nothing to prove

and nothing to hide. These are plain, humble, common birds and yet they build their nests in the presence of God. I will give birth in the presence of God. He, the Almighty, will be present to welcome this precious tiny baby into the world. He will make this valley of mourning into a place of springs – what will that look like for us? People will experience the goodness and faithfulness – the glory – of God through our reactions to the life of this child. I will be ever praising you, no matter what happens. Our faith will go from strength to strength.

No good thing does he withhold
from those whose way of life is blameless.
(Psalm 84:11b)

He will not withhold life from this baby.

I can't answer the question why some people experience healing and restoration and others don't. This is a mystery and a tension we live with. The reality is we live in a broken and fallen world, because each one of us sins and hurts other people and the environment around us. Sometimes we cry out for healing and God says yes; other times those prayers seem to be met with silence. We don't have the reasons why, but we can trust in the goodness and sovereignty of God, that only He knows the end from the beginning, only He knows what good could come from suffering. At that moment, I had faith and a mother's intuition in her baby's vitality that death might not come quickly for us.

One of the quandaries I could not reconcile was whether we would try again, after this baby.

I had it firmly in my mind that we would be a family of five. I had envisioned us having three children.

Yet during this pregnancy, drowning in the sickness and wretchedness of the first trimester, I'd promised myself, deep down, that I would never do this again. I just knew I didn't have it in me to endure extreme morning sickness one more time.

Before I'd been pregnant, I had no idea quite how long nine months can feel. There is no point from conception to birth when you are not pregnant, where you can set aside the bump and all the aches and symptoms it so generously bestows and regain a sense of your individual self. That baby is in your womb 24/7.

Every time you move or get dressed or look in the mirror, it is there. When you try to ease yourself behind the wheel of a car or slip between two objects, it is there.

I enjoyed going swimming during the final trimester of my first pregnancy and found that, for a short period of time, I felt like a dolphin in the water. The buoyancy of the water made me feel light and agile, yet as soon as I dragged myself out of the water, it was back to feeling like a whale.

I had experienced a new symptom this pregnancy: hypersalivation. One evening after brushing my teeth, my mouth continued to fill with saliva and I had to spit it out, again and again. It took a long time to get to sleep and I was horrified in the morning to find it didn't stop. I had to carry around tissues to spit into constantly, developed sore lips from wiping them and was rather self-conscious in public about my perpetual need to spit.

On the one hand, I felt done with being pregnant, and yet I could only imagine our household as a family of five. I knew there would always be an empty space, a missing person, if we were four. I know a lot of families find comfort in a rainbow baby – a baby born after any kind of baby loss. There is no hint the rainbow baby replaces the baby no longer with us, as each child is their own person, but having those empty arms full again can help.

After mulling on the quandary, I said to Paul one day, 'If we lose this baby early and never meet them alive, I might need to try again, to fill the space. But if this baby lives, even for a few days, I think that'll be it for me. That'll be our third baby and our family will be complete.'

We had to wait to see.

24
Baby clothes

18th January 2022

Preparing clothes for a newborn is part of the nesting process and it pained me that we weren't prepared for this little one. Our boxes of clothes stored in the shed were not, and might never be, suitable. 'Newborn' or 'up to one month' baby clothes are designed to fit a baby weighing seven pounds, and this baby was estimated to be three or four pounds at most. Even if the baby were born sleeping, I knew I wanted a set of clothes to dress them in and take photos together as a family. It felt like a semblance of normality and the ability to do something a mother would normally do and take for granted hundreds of times over (often with multiple changes in a day with leakages from one end or the other).

I had looked online and all of the tiny baby clothes seemed to be gendered: either pink or blue. We still didn't know if this baby was a boy or a girl and I wasn't going to buy both, so I would finish my searches feeling frustrated and discouraged. Providing clothes for my baby felt terribly important to me and it wasn't clear how I could do this.

One morning midweek, while both children were in preschool, I popped into my local supermarket. I had decided to buy Size 0 nappies and wet wipes for the baby, as an act of faith that they would need them, and while I was in the shop, I felt a pull to go and look at the baby clothes there. I had hardly bought any clothes for my two as we'd been lucky enough to receive lots of good-quality hand-me-downs and clothes as presents from family members, so I had never looked there before.

As I scanned the packaged items, one label caught my eye and my heart: Tiny Baby (<5lbs). I took a sharp breath in and quickly looked through the whole section, pulling out anything with that label. Incredibly, the vests were all white and the outfits, which were decidedly cute, were unisex also! The colours were pastel green and yellow and orange and featured cute elephants and other animals. Not only were they the right size, but they were also unisex – and I liked the style. It was like I'd received a personalised gift from heaven, right there in the back corner of the store. It was an emotional moment because it meant I could provide this baby with something that a mother should be able to – I could clothe him or her. I could dress them and keep them warm, even if I couldn't feed them myself.

In that moment, I knew I would always keep those tiny little outfits. They meant more to me than just a few sets of clothes. They were a sign to me that God knows what I need or even just deeply desire, and in His timing (which may not always feel right to us), He would give it. He also knew better than I did what this baby would need, and when, and I could trust Him. I paused for a moment after I had added the clothes to my basket, feeling discouragement dissipate and peace take its place. *I don't need to sort everything; He will. I don't need to source everything; He will. I don't need to know everything; He already does. I am not the only one fighting for my baby's life; He is.*

As I went up to the self-service checkouts, I had to wait for a member of staff to take the tags off the clothes.

'Oh, these are so cute!' she crooned. 'Such a lovely gift! So tiny, though; is the baby premature?'

'No, no. The baby's not been born yet,' I replied, mystified, as I stood there with a large, protruding belly.

'Ah, do they know if it's a boy or a girl yet?'

'Um, nope. No, they want to wait until it's born.' I wasn't sure how to respond.

'Lovely, well, I'm sure they'll love these,' and off she bustled to the next customer.

This member of staff thought I was buying a gift for someone else, whereas God was providing a gift for me: potentially the only sets of clothes my baby might ever wear. I could only say, 'Thank You, God.'

25
Late January

19th January 2022

My next scan was preceded by meeting the bereavement midwife in the Forget-Me-Not suite. It's set up with a bed, a couch and an en-suite shower room, retaining the easily wipeable surfaces obligatory in hospital settings but attempting to remove the harsh, clinical atmosphere with some soft touches. I sat on the sofa and she pulled up a chair as we discussed how I was coping, what I was feeling and the service she provides. She was able to offer three months of bereavement counselling, and it quickly became apparent that we helpfully shared the same faith. I was grateful for the bereavement midwife's support, and the knowledge she'd be sticking alongside us in those potentially difficult early months.

After meeting her, I went downstairs to the antenatal department for my next appointment, equipped with a book and some breakfast. I'd barely taken a bite when I was called in and flustered to get my book, container, phone and water bottle back in my bag and grab my hat, gloves and coat to scuttle into the consultant's room. We discussed the consultation with the specialist, as their letter had recently arrived.

'They're saying they recommend delivery at thirty-nine weeks,' she commented. 'That seems a bit late to me for such a small baby.'

'Thirty-nine weeks?' I echoed.

Anxiety twisted in my gut. It surely was an error to suggest waiting so long, but it felt a significant one. Or, I wondered, did the specialist think the timing of birth was of little consequence if the baby was going to die anyway? Well, it mattered hugely to me – it could mean the difference between life or death; between meeting this baby with its eyes open or permanently closed. I didn't want to wait until thirty-eight weeks; it felt far too risky.

Later that week, we emailed the neonatal consultant we'd talked with over Zoom to ask his advice on timing of delivery, and he replied to say an earlier delivery was safer, as there was more risk even from thirty-six to thirty-seven weeks. He reminded us small babies don't seem to do well being left in for longer. I found this decision profoundly difficult as it felt that, while others could advise, it really was down to us to make the call and, while the baby being born alive was our aim, we did want to allow the maximum amount of time for him or her to develop as fully as possible.

I got in contact with another charity that supports expectant parents who choose to continue a pregnancy with a life-limiting diagnosis, called Be Not Afraid.[24] They have an expert American neonatologist, affectionately known as Dr Marty, who offered to speak with us over Zoom. He graciously listened to our story and jumped in to say that each baby with Edwards' is unique, with different medical issues.

'If you've seen one baby with Edwards', then you've seen one baby with Edwards',' he told us. 'Each one is distinctive and presents with different symptoms so you need to consider this and individualise their care. It is good news that none of the markers seen is severe; I see no reason to presume right now that with standard medical care offered to any baby with normal chromosomes that your baby could not survive. And a natural birth might be OK, the baby seems to be strong.'

We explained how we felt pretty settled in our decision to have a C-section because we didn't want to take any risks, but did want his advice on the timing of delivery.

---

[24] www.benotafraid.net (accessed 13th November 2024).

'Well, the longer the baby is in, the more developed the lungs are, so ideally you might want to consider pushing to at least thirty-eight weeks, if all looks good, so the baby would be stronger and potentially more able to survive.'

Each person had given us slightly different advice and I felt lost in it all. In the end, we thought maybe we could propose a date towards the end of thirty-seven weeks and start of thirty-eight weeks, and see what the staff at the MDT thought.

'After receiving all this conflicting advice, I wouldn't be surprised if the baby decided to make an appearance in its own sweet time!' I joked with Paul. I have sometimes found in my Christian life that when a decision isn't clear and forthcoming, especially when I've prayed about it and waited on God for an answer, and when it's not an opportunity to use my own wisdom, that the choice ends up being taken out of my hands. Knowing this can lend a sense of peace as you release it from your control and trust things will work out, even if you don't (or can't) know what's best.

Dr Marty introduced us to a phrase we were to adopt as we moved forward in our planning for the birth: 'stabilise and evaluate'. He explained how, traditionally, babies with Edwards' were not offered any treatment at birth as they were expected to die, and so they often died quickly. It was a self-fulfilling prophecy. Studies show, however, that with interventions and treatment being given, the babies have a far better chance of surviving for longer.[25] He advised asking the team to stabilise the baby at birth, to help with breathing if needed, to take any other initial steps necessary and then to take time to evaluate what might be wrong, rather than assuming it would be a waste of time to intervene. Extending our time with our baby sounded glorious and we expressed our appreciation for his advice, expertise and wisdom, all given for free.

It wasn't only Dr Marty who was helpful from Be Not Afraid. Tracy – who was quick to point out that she is not a

[25] For example, www.pubmed.ncbi.nlm.nih.gov/38047023 (accessed 17th December 2024).

medical professional herself – is a parent care coordinator with more than ten years' experience. She asked me if I knew the difference between the sensitivity rate and the positive predictive value of the NIPT test for my specific age group. She commented, from reading my notes, that we did know for certain the baby had foetal growth restriction but we didn't know for sure that the baby had Edwards'. She sent me a link to an online calculator that works out, using maternal age and diagnosis rating, what the chance is that it is a false positive.

She wrote, 'Once there, you will see there is a 49% chance that your positive result is a false positive based on your age.'

I was thrown, once again.

The baby has it, the baby doesn't have it; the baby will die, the baby won't die.

It felt like I was a figure stuck in a child's game of imagination where the landscape of reality constantly shifted and changed shape, and I couldn't keep sight of what was real and what was pretend.

I quickly launched into research on my phone as to false positives for the NIPT test and was shocked to discover that while it is seen as highly accurate for Down syndrome, and is almost always accurate for negative results, there is a higher chance of false positives for T13 and T18 the older you get.

Could this mean there was an actual chance our baby didn't have it and it wasn't a delusional hope? And if they didn't, then was there another underlying reason why they were small and we were missing it because we'd got caught up with a false diagnosis? I didn't know whether to feel relieved or worried with a new collection of concerns.

26
MDT

27th January 2022

Before the MDT meeting, we emailed out our birth plan:

Baby Appleby Birth Plan

First of all, we want to thank you for the excellent ongoing care we have received from the hospital. We feel very supported and have appreciated meeting all of you.

This baby is our third – we have a four-year-old girl called Martha and a two-year-son called Jamie. We planned to have a third baby to complete our family and count the life of this child as precious, desired and sacred. Termination was never an option for us because we are committed Christians and see this baby as a gift from God.

Our priority is to meet this baby alive and we very much wish to minimise the risk of stillbirth if at all possible. We have not had an amniocentesis due to the potential risk and would prefer to deliver early to reduce the risk of foetal demise, at thirty-seven weeks. We do not know the gender of the baby because we wanted our last to be a surprise and so want that announcement of the gender to be a positive experience at birth. We have decided to have an elective C-section to give our baby the best chance of being born alive.

We would like the baby to be offered the standard initial resuscitation immediately after birth and active treatment continued until a decision can be made about prognosis. This is because we do not have a definite diagnosis of Trisomy 18 but a high likelihood given from the NIPT test. Because we are not 100 per cent sure of the diagnosis and because babies with T18 face a broad range of possible outcomes, we would like this baby to be offered life-sustaining interventions and assessed as to its condition before decisions are made as to palliative care. Around 5 to 10 per cent of babies with T18 live to a year old and we don't know if this baby might be one of those. If it is clear the baby will not live long, we will remove interventions and spend time making memories with the baby.

If Beth goes into spontaneous labour, we do not think we will want monitoring or an emergency C-section. We plan to let nature take its course and pray for life. Beth's previous labours were short – five hours for the first and two and a half hours for the second – so we think the priority will be making it to the hospital in time!

For an elective C-section, we would appreciate that happening as close to thirty-seven weeks as possible. We'd like to have steroid injections to support the baby's lungs. For both birth scenarios, we would appreciate as close to a hypnobirthing environment as possible, with low lighting and music playing.

Paul will accompany the baby after birth and would like to be involved in decisions made. We would like the baby to be offered resuscitation, to be stabilised after birth, given oxygen, IV fluids and an NG tube fitted if needed.[26] We would like to have genetic testing to confirm the diagnosis of Trisomy 18. We would like the baby to be admitted to SCBU if it seems likely to survive initially and then we will decide when to move to the hospice. Our current desire is to be moved to the hospice as soon as Beth is able so that our children can meet the baby.

In case of confirmed foetal demise, we will plan for an induction at the Forget-Me-Not room in the hospital with a move to the hospice as soon as possible. We would like the gender announcement to be made at birth and the baby to be placed on Mum's chest. We would like time to be

[26] A nasogastric tube goes through the nose and down the throat to deliver food and medicine directly into the stomach.

alone with the baby and all the memory-making items – we assume at the hospice, rather than the hospital.

We do reserve the right to change our minds about these requests at any point, as this is such a unique experience and we do not know how we'll feel at the time.

We would like the baby's grandparents to be able to visit if restrictions allow and possibly also our pastor, to dedicate the baby.

One winter afternoon, we gathered in a room in the Education Centre, a building on the same site as, but separate from, the main hospital. I had spent a few days drafting a birth plan then adding amendments from Paul and the neonatal consultant.

Attending the meeting were Sarah, the specialist nurse who'd given us a tour of SCBU, the matron of the Delivery Suite, our home-birth midwife, the bereavement midwife and two members of staff from the hospice: a doctor and a nurse from the SPACE (specialist paediatric palliative care) team. Notable absences included our foetal medicine consultant, whom I had expected to be there but was on leave, and anyone from the obstetrics team, even though they'd been included on the emails.

We sat around a large table and everyone had a copy of the birth plan in front of them, which I was grateful for, as it provided the initial introduction for us and made our desires clear. Sarah chaired the meeting and, overall, everyone was onboard with our wish to 'stabilise and evaluate' at birth.

'We don't know for sure that this baby does have Edwards',' I pointed out, wanting everyone to give our baby a chance and not write them off. Even babies with full Edwards' deserve a chance at life, but I knew how much drive goes into sustaining a sick baby's life if the odds of them making a full recovery are higher.

'Well, we do really know for sure, though, don't we?' was the reply I received.

I didn't push back. I wish I had.

A lot of scenarios were discussed, with decisions we'd need to make, and we responded to most with the desire to sustain life, except for ventilation. It did pain me to agree to any treatment being withheld from my baby, but I took solace in the fact we'd asked for the grace to be able to change our minds at any point.

I remember one question being asked that was so strange, I couldn't quite believe it: 'If the baby gets an infection, you'd have to decide whether or not to treat it.' I was so thrown, I didn't formulate a proper answer.

'I'm sorry?' I wish I had replied. 'Are you asking me if we'd like to provide effective medicine for a treatable condition? Why would we not?'

It was a sign to me that even if the medical world think they've moved on from 'comfort care' and letting a baby die, their basic outlook was still the same. If someone with terminal cancer got an infection, would you query giving them antibiotics? I didn't understand how this could even be a question. No, I didn't want my baby to die of an infection that could have been treated just to speed up the process of dying.

There was discussion around timing of birth, and eventually it was settled that we'd plan for a C-section at thirty-seven weeks plus four days, which was a Monday in late February. All the team we'd need would be on hand, and everyone could be prepared. It was agreed I'd come in for regular CTGs (cardiotocography) to monitor the baby's heart rate from thirty-six weeks onwards, to check how the baby was doing and pick up any signs of distress.

Someone joked, 'Whatever happens, you don't want an emergency C-section late on a Friday evening. Monday morning is best so you have a full week of medical staff being on hand, rather than a smaller crew over the weekend.'

The matron was extraordinarily kind and said that if I went into spontaneous labour, she'd come round herself to help deliver the baby as she lived near us. She also told us, if we were in the hospital and didn't have much time, they'd get our kids into the Forget-Me-Not room to allow them to meet the baby. She definitely gave me the impression she was championing us and would shift protocol if need be to make things work in our favour. I could understand how she'd won personal awards and recognition for her exceptional care.

The biggest news to me in that meeting came after I asked a fairly simple question: 'What would happen if Paul or I got Covid?'

As the country had started to open up and mask-wearing was no longer obligatory, the danger of us catching the virus had increased. I was not prepared for the answer.

'If you test positive for Covid before the birth, then you can still deliver here at the hospital, but I'm afraid the baby won't be able to go into SCBU because of the risk to the other babies.'

'The same is true for the hospice, I'm sorry to say. We can't let anyone with a confirmed case of Covid enter as it would endanger the children, as well as the staff.

'If Paul tests positive for Covid, he won't be able to be with you at the delivery.'

I was horrified. Potentially catching this virus, which we'd managed to dodge for almost two years now, could derail all of our plans for birth. The thought that Paul might not be present for the birth and therefore potentially miss meeting the baby or being present for decisions about interventions and care after birth was not worth thinking about. The same with not being able to access the hospice, the thought of which was sustaining us with its anticipation of complete wraparound care.

We made the decision then and there to isolate completely for the two weeks prior to birth. I told the children's preschool that they wouldn't be coming in the week after half term, and Paul requested to not see patients the first week but to work alone in a room in the surgery, and then booked the second week off as annual leave. We could not take any chances. It was not worth it.

27
Instagram post

30th January 2022

You don't take many bump photos when it's not your first, but I realised I'd regret not having any this time round. So here I am, thirty-three weeks, holding on to hope.

Hope feels dangerous.

Hope makes you vulnerable.

Hoping for a good outcome leaves you wide open to disappointment and devastation if the worst happens.

Holding on to hope is risky.

It can feel easier to lower your expectations, live with the fear, the anxiety, the pessimism.

Prepare yourself for the worst and so minimise the damage inflicted.

Does that even work?

What if hoping allows your heart to soar above the mundane of this world? To see the glorious colours and experience the wide-open spaces of dreaming?

What if hope creeps in unawares when you're not protecting your heart and invites anticipation of good?

Do you squash it, eliminate it or allow it to bloom and blossom?

We each have a choice.

I may be afraid of what the next month holds, feeling increasingly emotional as we approach the delivery date, but I am choosing HOPE.

> May the God of hope fill you with all joy and peace as you trust in him, so that you may overflow with hope by the power of the Holy Spirit.
> (Romans 15:13)

28
Nightmare

29th January 2022

> The distresses of my heart increase;
> bring me out of my sufferings.
> (Psalm 25:17, CSB)

I woke up in the middle of the night, distraught. I couldn't shake the feeling of distress from my dream and started to cry. It wasn't a dream, really, but a nightmare. It had started with the four of us queuing in some sort of immigration processing centre, waiting to be let in to a new country. For some reason, the adults were separated from the children and let in first. I assumed Martha and Jamie would be taken care of but felt anxious at being apart, so I returned to the centre to find them. As I searched and searched, a mounting sense of dread and panic filled me. When I did find them, my relief was immense. They were alone and uncared for, but were actually fine. The predominant feelings I was left with were the horror of being apart and then the incredible, overwhelming relief of being reunited with them, knowing they were back, safe with me, where they belonged.

It made me wonder if, deep down, I knew there was little I could do to protect this baby and keep him or her safe and that was distressing me. It also made me realise that I didn't know how long I'd be away from the children when I had the C-section, and if I might end up not seeing them for a few days. I knew I wouldn't be discharged for at least twenty-four hours, but I wondered if they could come and visit me. Jamie hadn't

140

been apart from me for more than three hours, the length of a morning at preschool, and I'd never had a night away from either of them. How would they cope if Mummy suddenly disappeared for a few days?

Another thought occurred to me: what if the baby had a prolonged stay in SCBU and I was torn between spending time with them there, potentially the only time I might spend with them in this life, and being at home with my other children, attempting to retain a sense of normality for them? The time with the baby may be heartbreakingly limited but I couldn't neglect the kids.

It never occurred to me that the baby I was carrying might actually be fine too and might cause me to experience immense relief.

I didn't even let myself think about if one of us caught Covid and we had do this journey alone. That was a worry I didn't need and wouldn't entertain. As my father would say, 'We'll cross that bridge when we come to it,' and I chose to believe we wouldn't come to it.

30th January 2022

The next day at church, a young mother a few rows in front of us stood up after feeding her baby and put him over her shoulder to burp him. His contented little milk-drunk face and the confident ease of her movements brought to the surface a desire deep in me: *I want my newborn. I want my baby!*

Anticipatory grief hit me like a bullet train in that moment, ploughing right through my carefully constructed cardboard barriers and sweeping my emotional stability away. As much as I'd struggled with those early months of sleep deprivation and the difficulties breastfeeding with my other two, I wanted this again! I was desperate for all those taken-for-granted moments I'd had daily with the other two and felt ripped apart at the thought of not having them with my third.

My emotional roller coaster continued, throwing loops and turns I couldn't have anticipated, lifting and dropping me without warning. I wondered how someone without a faith in a good God and a glorious heaven might go through this kind of ordeal without experiencing depression or drowning in hopelessness. It seemed beyond me, as I needed daily reassurance in prayer and reading encouraging Scriptures to keep me from sinking.

I spoke with a friend later about her experience in the hospital, and she told me her daughter wasn't allowed to visit when she was in after her C-section, but that she had been discharged the next day. What if I needed to be in longer and I couldn't see the children at all?

As all these feelings and fears had built up by late that day, I took time to pray and breathe deeply and try to reassure myself: *I am never alone and this baby isn't going to die. The children will be fine and well taken care of. God will look after us all.*

I prayed fervently that day for the baby to not have a cleft palate or anything wrong with its heart. I wanted it to be a mistake, all a terrible mistake.

Also, searching online, I'd found some baby clothes even smaller than the supermarket ones. A well-known high-street brand was selling pure cotton premature sleepsuits and vests for babies who weigh three to four pounds. They had poppers all round the edge and flaps for the feet to make it easier to keep oxygen monitor straps on or to take a baby's temperature. If I were to buy these, was it in faith that the baby would need multiple sets of clothes, or was it a delusional hope and then the lack of their use might be a sore reminder of what had been taken away?

My verse that day was, 'The LORD is my strength and my shield; my heart trusts in him, and he helps me' (Psalm 28:7a). I repeated it to myself and allowed the truth of His care to cover me and settle in my heart, dampening down the constant questions and concerns.

1st February 2022

The following day, my prayers were guided by the next psalm: 'The voice of the LORD is powerful; the voice of the LORD is majestic' (Psalm 29:4).

My prayer was for the voice of the Lord to speak life over this baby. The Psalms anchored me in what and how to pray and gave daily guidance on how to keep interceding for our child. Often, when you're the one in the middle of a crisis, you don't know how to pray, you don't have words to speak and feel at sea as to how to even begin. You need others to lower you down through the roof to Jesus' feet or to keep holding up your outstretched arms when you've no strength left.[27] Written prayers or verses from the Bible can give you those words sometimes, and allow the desire and emotion to be channelled into expression.

One thing I found it tricky to pray about was having a child with complex medical needs. If I (most of the time) had faith that this baby might live, then what kind of care might they need, and how would we be able to provide that when we already had two small children? This was a new area for faith and trust in God. It wasn't as simple as the dichotomy between life and death. It was trusting God with an ongoing difficult future where I could be stretched beyond my current capacity and forced to find new ways to cope and new support structures to carry us; where my children would have to learn new levels of being independent; and where our understanding of what it looked like to care for those in need would have to crack open and expand exponentially. Now it wouldn't be a neatly packaged time-restricted caring for others that suited our schedule and preferences. It would be round the clock, inconvenient and intrusive. It'd be part of us; it'd be family.

I received a text message from my home-birth midwife later that day responding to my question about whether the children could visit in the hospital, and she replied to say yes, because

---

[27] Luke 5:17-26; Exodus 17:8-13.

we'd be in the Forget-Me-Not room, and special exceptions could be made there because they wouldn't have to enter the delivery suite. That put my heart at rest. I wouldn't be away from them too long. It was a comforting thought.

While those concerns subsided, as the next appointment approached, new worries started to bubble up. What if the baby had stopped growing and they wanted to deliver now? Would the baby be strong enough to survive? How many weeks would they remain in hospital?

Once again, I found I needed to take my attention off the storm raging around me and instead focus on the words of God and the person of Jesus. He is the only one who can keep us afloat when waves threaten to pull us under. It's not easy to keep Truth in the centre of your attention, rather than allowing the fear to overtake, but I found it worth the effort. Memorising Scripture gave me an opportunity to meditate on the words and allow the meaning to blossom and take root in my soul. I found faith doesn't mean pretending hard things aren't happening or expecting them to disappear because I'd prayed. Instead, it was making a choice to trust that God would show His goodness through it all as I acknowledged the pain with Him, and knew in my soul He'd carry me through, even when I could no longer stand.

2nd February 2022

I changed the focus of my psalm for this day to make it a prayer:

> LORD my God, I called to you for help,
> and you healed [my baby].
> You, LORD, brought [my baby] up from the realm of the dead,
> you spared [my baby] from going down to the pit …
>
> To you, LORD, I called;
> to the Lord I cried for mercy:
> 'What is gained if [my baby is] silenced,
> if [my baby goes] down to the pit?

Will the dust praise you?
Will it proclaim your faithfulness?
Hear, LORD, and be merciful to me;
LORD, be my help.'

You turned my wailing into dancing;
you removed my sackcloth[28] and clothed me with joy,
that my heart may sing your praises and not be silent.
LORD my God, I will praise you for ever.
(Psalm 30:2-3, 8-12)

I wrote in my diary, after copying down that passage:

Starting to realise there are times in life which are like
markers, where you see for real if you trust God, or you
realise you don't. 'Is God actually good?' is a question that
really matters, and your answer colours your interpretation
of reality. I have faith this baby will live and I have peace.
A lot of people are praying for us and so I know I am being
carried on their prayers. But, no matter what does happen,
I also recognise that I do trust God. I know He is good and
His desire for my family is good.

This assurance was helped by the fact that the scan that day had
been fine. The baby was head down, low in the pelvis, which is
a good position for late pregnancy as it means they're
positioning themselves ready for birth. More importantly, the
current measurements made the baby's estimated weight around
three pounds, making him or her bigger than had been initially
expected. That seemed positive to me and I was willing to take
any good news available.

4th February 2022

I will be glad and rejoice in your love,
for you saw my affliction
and knew the anguish of my soul.
(Psalm 31:7)

---

[28] Mourning clothes.

Diary entry:

I'm coming to realise I have a choice in how these last few weeks of pregnancy go – possibly my last month of being pregnant ever. I could be fearful, counting down the days, dwelling on worst-case scenarios, grieving in advance – or we could have fun, appreciate every day we know this baby is safe in my womb, kicking and wriggling, trusting the Lord for the future we can neither see nor predict, taking each day as it comes and knowing God'll be with us no matter what happens. You don't dispel fear by safeguarding from the worst happening but by knowing God'll take you through even exactly that happening and you'll survive. The comfort of God is very real.

A charity in the States set up by a lovely lady called Jen Stolz, whose baby Zoe Faith had anencephaly, is giving us money for trips out to make memories before the baby is born. To help change this from a season of mourning to one of celebration. It has also financed the soft penguin teddy I've recorded the baby's heartbeat on to.

The kids never got dressed today. We didn't leave the house. I spent the rainy dismal morning cleaning and tidying the downstairs floor as they played. As I was cleaning the inside of the microwave, I realised, 'I'm nesting.' It was prompted by a sudden need to get things sorted and ready for the baby. And I did order those tiny premature vests.

My dear baby, I'm getting ready to welcome you into this world. Please arrive safely and please arrive breathing.

6th February 2022

Instagram post:

What if we don't spend our energy worrying over and trying to prevent our worst-case scenarios from happening but look those monsters straight in the eye and say, 'I'm not afraid of you.'

'I'm not afraid of you. You can't break me. You can't strip me of the things that matter most because I will always, always be beloved of the Lord, always have His presence and His comfort near me, always know my eternity is secure with Him and, no matter what evil this world throws at me, none of the mud will stick. I will not become bitter or angry or pessimistic; I will not believe the worst of people or never give them the benefit of the doubt.'

How could I survive in a world where God isn't good and doesn't always intend good for us? Yes, He allows the consequences of our selfish actions to play out, causing unimaginable pain and sorrow, but what is love if it's not a choice? It cannot be forced. So He gives us the option of trusting and believing in Him and His goodness, experiencing His comfort and closeness through the darkest nights, or walking away and pursuing our own paths.

So I choose to trust. Not that everything is going to work out fine and I'll never face pain or grief or sorrow. But that His love and compassion and kindness will wrap around me, showing the beauty in the brokenness because He is near. The comfort of presence. Of empathy. That death is not the end and we will one day be reunited, for eternity. In glory.

#34weekspregnant #countingdown #stillaliveandkicking #hope

29
Early February

6th February 2022

> You are my hiding-place;
> you will protect me from trouble
> and surround me with songs of deliverance.
> (Psalm 32:7)

Martha made up a song at bedtime about putting flowers on the baby. We'd walked through a church graveyard in a neighbouring town centre the previous day, where she'd spotted a bunch of flowers laid in remembrance on a grave, and asked us why there were flowers on the ground.

'Has someone dropped them? Did they forget they'd left them there?' she questioned us.

We attempted to explain that these were graves and people who'd died were buried underneath. We continued to say that the family and friends who missed them sometimes left flowers as a gift to show their love and to remember them.

'Will we leave flowers on the ground when the baby dies, Mummy?' she asked.

I swallowed hard in an attempt to dispel the tightness in my throat and tried to answer honestly.

'Yes, Martha, we probably will.'

These were her lyrics, a four-year-old's way of making sense of her world: 'Cover him with flowers, Mummy and Daddy's baby, God can do that.' Her innocence and care filled and pained my heart.

In church that day, a friend had preached on Romans 5:3-4 and I wrote those verses in my diary too: 'Not only so, but we also glory in our sufferings, because we know that suffering produces perseverance; perseverance, character; and character, hope.'

We had a very real Hope we were holding out for, a real-life breathing and crying one, or a Daniel David. Whichever one came.

I had an idea about calling for a day of worship on the day the baby was to be born and of asking people to surround us with 'songs of deliverance' (Psalm 32:7). The news had been full of a huge rescue mission launched for a five-year-old Moroccan boy who'd fallen down a well,[29] and it clearly showed how everyone agrees that the life of one child has immense value. So I felt we could raise a trumpet call to launch a massive prayer-focused rescue mission for the life of this child. I felt the day they were born would be critical, and I prayed other people would catch this vision and run with it.

7th February 2022

> But the eyes of the LORD are on those who fear him,
> on those whose hope is in his unfailing love,
> to deliver them from death
> and keep them alive in famine.
>
> We wait in hope for the LORD;
> he is our help and our shield.
> In him our hearts rejoice,
> for we trust in his holy name.
> May your unfailing love be with us, LORD,
> even as we put our hope in you.
> (Psalm 33:18-22)

Nesting carried on the next day as Paul and I hoovered and dusted the whole house, bagged up and stored away all the

---

[29] www.bbc.co.uk/news/av/world-africa-60267514 (accessed 17th December 2024).

grown-out-of clothes and put a too-small car seat into the loft. I repacked the hospital bag, with baby clothes and nappies and wet wipes this time, just in case, and made a list of the items I'd need to pack last minute.

I wondered if this intense nesting was the baby's way (through my own body) of preparing me for an earlier arrival than planned. Or did I have in the back of my mind that the final weeks might be taken up with hospital visits and CTGs and blood tests, so I wanted to get ready ahead of time? Of course, the house would need another clean before the planned C-section, but I needed to feel I could keep on top of things, rather than feeling swamped by all the outstanding jobs.

8th February 2022

> I sought the LORD, and he answered me;
> he delivered me from all my fears.
> (Psalm 34:4)

I couldn't help noticing my verse of the day didn't say, 'He gave me the ability to overcome my fears.' No, it says, 'he *delivered* me from all my fears':[30] our fears can be too much for us to handle and we sometimes need to be saved from them. Like a person thrown overboard in a storm or stuck in a burning building, there are times we need to be rescued, and no self-help mantra will get us out of those emergencies ourselves. We often need to keep asking for deliverance, until we're living in peace, and not settle for being delivered from some fear but not *all* fears. The Bible promises peace that 'surpasses all understanding' which will 'guard [our] hearts and minds' (Philippians 4:7, NKJV). It might not mean we're being rescued from the anxiety-inducing situation or challenging time, but we discover we can remain in peace through it all.

I ended the day physically exhausted. I'd walked down to preschool and back twice, which was too much for my pelvic

---

[30] My italics.

pain. I'd walked with Paul in the morning and then my dear friend Rowena in the afternoon, with her staying until the kids were tucked up in bed. I relied on her and other friends from church, like Aunty Jo, who came round regularly when Paul was working late, to help me with teatime, bath time and bedtime. Doing this alone would cause stress and angst, I reasoned, so why not have help if it made it an enjoyable and calmer experience? We all benefited from Rowena's and Jo's wisdom, input and friendship, so the more time we got with them, the better. They became part of our family.

9th February 2022

> The eyes of the LORD are on the righteous,
> and his ears are attentive to their cry …
>
> The LORD is close to the broken-hearted
> and saves those who are crushed in spirit.
> (Psalm 34:15, 18)

This evening we had our last Expectant Family Zoom call with the SOFT UK community. It was only one other couple and ourselves. All of the others we'd journeyed with so far had had their babies; some lived a few weeks but all now had passed. It was sobering to only be us. It was a privilege to journey with others through such a dark and difficult chapter of their lives, but it was hard.

10th-13th February 2022

I seemed to run out of energy by the end of the week, which was unfortunate because Paul had an online course all Saturday morning and had agreed to take an extra work shift on Sunday morning. I felt we hadn't planned that well when I was woken by the children in the early hours and then couldn't get back to sleep. 'Discouraged, emotional, low' was how I described myself that day in my diary; 'uncomfortable and miserable – like death warmed up' was how I felt.

I'd been worried about shooting pain and discomfort, only for a midwife to explain to me these are normal symptoms for a third pregnancy, when the pelvic floor isn't what it used to be. Emotionally and physically, I was drained.

At one point over the weekend, when I was alone with the kids, I crept into bed while they played nearby, and any time they thought I might have fallen asleep, they poked me in the face to make sure I was awake. One night, my bump was so sore I had to take paracetamol to get to sleep and looked forward to the day I could take ibuprofen again.

I sent out a long update to our WhatsApp prayer group, being honest about how I was feeling and sharing 'Raise a Hallelujah' by Jonathan and Melissa Helser,[31] a song written out of a prayer time for a small boy who was on the brink of death. I asked for prayer coverage for the upcoming appointments and shared how we'd be isolating for the next couple of weeks or so.

> Take delight in the LORD,
> and he will give you the desires of your heart.
> (Psalm 37:4)

[31] Jonathan David Helser, Melissa Helser, 'Raise a Hallelujah', Bethel Music; www.youtube.com/watch?v=G2XtRuPfaAU (accessed 13th November 2024).

30
The hospice

14th February 2022

> All my longings lie open before you, Lord;
> my sighing is not hidden from you …
>
> LORD, I wait for you;
> you will answer, Lord my God.
> (Psalm 38:9, 15)

The time came for us to visit the children's hospice, an incredible purpose-built facility. It supports families of children with life-limiting conditions by providing respite care, specialist nursing and a wide range of activities and events. We were taking Martha and Jamie with us, and we'd been assured there would be staff available to look after them while we were meeting to discuss the Symptom Management Plan.

I had geared myself up for this to be a heavy day, as we would be discussing what care and medication we might want this baby to receive if they got poorly quite quickly. I didn't want to be thinking about this, but I also knew we needed a plan in place, even as we hoped for a better outcome.

We drove up, put on face masks and entered. I was so impressed by the hospice. It seemed a genuinely lovely place to be, as well as highly professional, full of experience and expertise. The children also had a whale of a time.

We started with a tour and were astonished at the variety of what was offered and how everything seemed to be taken care of. There were residential rooms downstairs for a baby or child to be cared for individually, opening out on to the extensive garden filled with outdoor toys and playground equipment. I could tell Martha and Jamie were keen to get out and play, even in winter temperatures. We saw the family flats upstairs where we could all stay if we wanted to, and the large dining room where meals were provided.

There was a hydrotherapy pool we didn't get to see as it was in use, a little soft play our kids definitely did use, an arts and games area, a music studio, a tranquil suite, a complimentary therapy room and a teenagers' den.

A few specific things remain in my memory because I had an aversion to them being used for my baby. One was a cold room, where a body can be stored at a low-enough temperature for preservation, yet still be accessible in those first few days of bereavement. Another was the framed hand and footprints on display as an example piece, and I remember a strong desire rising up: 'I don't want a picture of my child's hands or feet; I want their real, warm hands and feet that keep growing and aren't stuck at one size forever.'

And finally, the piece that had me in sudden and inescapable tears: the memory garden and, in particular, the tree of remembrance. Set in a secluded, peaceful courtyard in the centre of the complex were three wooden benches circling a mirrored table with a large glass orb. Green foliage of varying heights cuddled the benches from behind and circled the table, adding to the sense of beauty and calm. We were led to one structure where delicate metal leaves hung from the branches, twirling and dancing in the breeze: the tree of remembrance. Every little leaf had the name on it of a child who had died, and I suddenly and desperately didn't want my child's name on that tree. As beautiful and precious as this piece was, I wanted no part of it. I couldn't speak from the welling emotion, and the member of staff accompanying us gave me a hug and a moment to recover.

Once the tour was completed, we headed to the garden and the children were let loose in the Wendy houses outside, while we met with a doctor and a nurse to talk through a document produced for our baby. I found the discussion quite medical, and it enabled me to distance this from the baby prodding my ribs as we talked. I felt myself slip fully into 'head' mode where I could function with the information we were discussing and keep my heart from getting involved. These weren't scenarios that would actually happen, I kept telling myself; it was all just another scene in the dark game of imagination we were trapped in.

They handed over a typed, detailed care plan with various scenarios that might play out, including the baby being born at home, a lengthy stay in hospital and the baby being brought to the hospice, with lists of medication that would be administered to relieve any pain they might be in. I let Paul be the main person in this discussion, as he knew what these pain meds were, and I trusted their knowledge and expertise. It was all theory to me, and therefore felt light and removed from my reality. I was fine with this coping strategy of not having to visualise what these scenarios would look like with a real-life baby that I loved.

When our discussion was over, with the care plan updated and sent to the hospital to be added to our notes, we went to find the kids. They didn't want to leave. They'd been happily playing with two family support workers and felt there was still so much more of the building to explore.

'We might be coming back here soon enough,' I said, in an attempt to encourage them to leave. 'We might be staying here for a little while after the baby is born.'

They thought this sounded great, but still wanted a few more minutes to play. Paul, in his irrepressible style, quickly created a throwing and catching game with the kids, and didn't give me an option not to join. Unfortunately, my throwing and catching skills leave much to be desired, and I managed to throw a ball straight into Jamie's face and he instantly started wailing.

'Alright, time to leave!'

My parents arrived that afternoon for what we assumed would be an extended stay. We needed their help with the children while I was attending various appointments at the hospital, all

155

now coming with greater frequency as we neared the end. Unacknowledged was the need for them to be on hand for any sudden emergency or contractions starting.

Martha made us all chuckle over dinner when she authoritatively declared, 'I don't like babies.'

As much as we hoped this baby would come home, there was one member of the family who liked to keep them as a concept and not a reality. Disliking loud noises, she'd not been a fan of Jamie when we brought him home and she had swiftly left the room any time he cried. Now she was older, I had been curious to see how both of them would respond to a younger sibling. It was desperately sad that I didn't know if I would ever find out.

15th February 2022

Facebook update:

> For those of you who don't know, Paul & I are expecting our third child. As much as we find parenting crazy challenging at times, our kids bring us so much joy and we felt our family wasn't quite finished yet. Unfortunately this pregnancy has been the hardest yet with awful morning sickness (yet again) and limiting pelvic pain. And then the 20-week scan revealed some issues.

> What was said to us: 'Your baby has a genetic condition called Trisomy 18, or Edward's syndrome, which is incompatible with life. I fully expect your baby to die in the womb. If your baby survives pregnancy and birth, then it will die within hours or days. I know you've said you don't want a termination, but you can change your mind at any point in the pregnancy, right up to birth.'

> What I wish had been said: 'I'm sorry to tell you it looks like your baby has a genetic condition called Trisomy 18, or Edward's syndrome, which is a life-limiting condition. Babies with this condition often pass away before birth but the longer the pregnancy progresses, the more chance they have to survive to full term. A small percentage, 5-10%, live

up to a year or more, but you may want to prepare for your baby to pass fairly soon after birth. You've said you don't want a termination so I won't mention it again.'

We're now at 36 weeks, have received incredible care and support from hospital & hospice staff, family & friends, charities & support organisations and we want this story to continue a little bit longer.

Please pray with us for life for this baby!

Diary entry:

I decided today it was the right time to put something on Facebook. It had felt too public and exposed before now, but for some reason, thirty-six weeks felt right. Like we've lasted the pregnancy and next will be the announcement of birth, and actually a whole lot more people are now praying. Great outcome.

I posted the update while I was at the hairdresser's and wasn't quite prepared for the comments and messages: an outpouring of kindness. A friend told me her first baby had had T18 and another said his niece had. No one has stories of babies living. Some said they have faith for a miracle; wouldn't that be incredible – if the baby came out small but totally fine? When would we know they were fine: straight away or once genetic testing results had come back? A cleft palate will be easy to confirm but I don't know about a heart condition.

But now, Lord, what do I look for?
My hope is in you.
(Psalm 39:7)

Last scan tomorrow. Definitely love feeling baby move around and poke and prod away. Keep fighting, my little one.

31
Final scan

16th February 2022

> I waited patiently for the LORD;
> he turned to me and heard my cry.
> (Psalm 40:1)

I woke with a throbbing headache at 3am and got up to take some paracetamol. It didn't help. An hour and a half later, I decided to see if sitting upright might help ease the pounding around my left eye socket.

'What time is it?' Paul asked sleepily, disturbed by my movement.

He then spent the next hour fetching me water, taking my blood pressure, massaging my shoulders and back, giving me hugs and praying for me. Eventually, it was a cold damp flannel across my forehead that gave me some relief. Inside, though, I was scared. My blood pressure, which is normally reliably average, had crept up to the threshold of concerningly high and I knew what that meant. A crippling headache and blood pressure going through the roof equal pre-eclampsia, and pre-eclampsia meant the baby was coming. I wasn't ready for that.

At 7am, another dose of paracetamol barely touched the pain, and when my blood pressure remained high, I knew I needed to phone the Pregnancy Advice Line.

As I explained the situation, I could hear my voice getting smaller and more high-pitched as my panic surfaced. The fear of what we were expecting seemed too real, too immediate. I wasn't ready for this baby to come now. I wasn't ready to meet him or her and say goodbye.

'You do need to go into hospital to be checked out, OK? They'll take good care of you and you don't need to worry right now. Take some deep breaths and try to keep calm. Yes, do take your hospital bag with you if you've got it packed, but don't worry if not – you can sort all those things out later,' the person on the end of the line tried to reassure me.

Grateful my parents were already there and could keep the kids to their normal routine, Paul reported his absence to work, then drove me in.

By 9am I was on the ward and, mercifully, my blood pressure there was registering within the normal range.

'Sometimes automatic monitors register a little high, whereas doing it manually seems to give a more accurate reading,' the midwife on the antenatal ward explained.

While the blood pressure had stabilised, my headache remained. I had to keep my eyes closed as light exacerbated it, and Paul kept refreshing the flannel with cold water.

I was hooked up to a CTG monitor and was asked for a urine sample and we sat and waited, watching the baby's heart rate zigzag on the reel of paper rotating out of the machine.

We were soon told the sample had registered some pluses in glucose and white blood cells, so it was being sent off for analysis.

The junior doctor came round and reassured me we weren't dealing with pre-eclampsia, so the baby could stay put a little longer. I found I was able to breathe a bit more easily.

'Is there any reason you think you might have this headache?' she asked me.

I almost couldn't reply, I was so taken aback by her question. I assume this was a question they'd been trained to ask, but I still couldn't help myself answering, 'Do you know my baby is supposed to have Edwards' syndrome? Do you know we've been told this baby is going to die? Do you think this might be causing me some stress?'

I genuinely didn't know if she knew! I didn't have access to the notes she had, and didn't know how much time she'd taken to read them beforehand.

I would like to add here that when I spoke about this baby, I was very, very careful in what I said and how I phrased it. Remembering my talk on James 3, I believe there is incredible power in our words, to create and to destroy, just like a marriage can be destroyed in one admission of infidelity, or a relationship can be created with a confession of love. God created this world through speech, and the Bible says, 'The tongue has the power of life and death' (Proverbs 18:21a).

I never said, 'My baby has Edwards' syndrome,' or, 'This baby is going to die.' As the mother, I knew my words had authority, so I never pronounced that reality. Instead, I always couched it in terms of having being given a diagnosis or having been told this was the case. For me, this was a way of providing protection and even hope through my words, albeit in a small way.

The doctor prescribed codeine, which was mercifully effective, and soon I was relieved of the headache.

The CTG, though, showed up some interesting things: every time the baby moved, their heart rate would accelerate, and there was one serious deceleration when I seemed to have a Braxton Hicks contraction, which I didn't feel. [32]

A deceleration, where the heart rate slows down considerably, is often an indicator of a baby being in distress. We took this as a clear sign we'd made the right choice to proceed with a C-section and not put the baby through natural labour, potentially causing them harm.

Once I was feeling better, Paul headed off to work, where his colleagues had covered his morning calls, and I was discharged and headed downstairs from the ward to the clinic.

---

[32] 'Braxton Hicks contractions are mild, irregular contractions during pregnancy', www.mayoclinichealthsystem.org/hometown-health/speaking-of-health/5-common-questions-about-braxton-hicks-contractions (accessed 17th December 2024).

I sat outside the consultant's room and waited for my regular scan, concerned I was seeing no one going in or out. She had said she didn't have an antenatal clinic when I was thirty-six weeks pregnant so she'd added me on to the end of her gynae clinic instead. When she eventually emerged from a different room, wearing scrubs and marching down the corridor, looking ready for her lunch break, I jumped up as quickly as I could, which turned out to be rather awkwardly at my size, and called to get her attention.

'Oh right, yes,' she replied. 'Was it today we were having that final scan?' She ushered me into the ultrasound room, turned the computers on and explained that new machines had arrived that week and she wasn't used to using them yet.

For five minutes, she swept the device over my belly, confirmed the baby still had a heartbeat and was moving around, and then we were done. No notes were made or measurements taken, and I remember thinking, 'She didn't even pull up my notes. How do we know if the baby is still growing if we don't plot the measurements on the graph?'

To be completely honest, right in that moment I hadn't wanted to know if the baby had stopped growing, as I didn't want to face what would happen if they had. I wanted the baby to stay in and, after all the palaver of the morning, I just wanted to go home and go to bed.

That was the end of the scans – the last time I'd see this baby in grainy black and white, moving about on a screen. I dearly hoped it wasn't the last time I would see them alive and active. This consultant had been so kind throughout our scans, letting us 'make memories' watching the baby moving around on the screen. She had tried to make it a positive experience and a time to bond, rather than only listing all that was wrong. Just as I was starting to feel safe in her room, now was the time to emerge from the chrysalis of pregnancy and face what was to come.

32
CTGs

18th February 2022

Storm Eunice swept across the UK and took some of our roof tiles with it. My father, sat in our loft room, heard the end ridge tile dislodge, cracking another tile on its way down, and then smash into pieces on the shared driveway. It would not have been a good time to be outdoors, so we kept the children sheltered inside.

Paul took me back to the hospital to the Planned Assessment Unit for the first scheduled CTG. With my previous pregnancies, a member of staff would hook me up, attaching monitors held in place with coloured straps to my belly, and then return after a period of time to look at the printout and declare if all was well or not. Nowadays, technology had advanced so that after anything between twelve minutes and an hour, the machine itself would decide if the baby was fine and a little light would turn from amber to green.

A reassuringly short twelve minutes later, the light had changed to indicate we were good to go, my blood pressure was fine and the glucose pluses in the urine were still present but were not seen as a concern any longer. I went home to rest.

I'd started to express colostrum, and froze tiny amounts of breast milk in little syringes in the dearly held hope that the baby would benefit from it. I didn't need to worry about starting too early in this pregnancy, as the concern of bringing labour on early wasn't present now. I wanted to do everything I could to give this baby the best possible start in life.

Put your hope in God,
for I will yet praise him,
my Saviour and my God.
(Psalm 42:11b)

21st February 2022

My next CTG kept me in hospital for three hours. A trace of protein in the urine prompted blood tests to check on liver and kidney function, and I was advised to stick around until those results were returned. In better news, my blood pressure was even lower and no infection had been found in the urine sent off the previous week. So I pottered around, getting myself a sandwich and a coffee and eventually was given the all-clear after midday.

Our pastor and his wife called round in the evening with a care package filled with carefully chosen presents, and it occurred to me that we were going to need more vases. We only had a few, received as wedding presents, and they were already being used. I suddenly thought, 'We might need more, a lot more.'

Prime Minister Boris Johnson announced that day all Covid restrictions would end in a few days' time, on Thursday 24th, so there would be no more isolating for the vulnerable, no more face masks in crowded places and free testing was ending soon.

This felt so out of sync with where we were at, as the NHS wasn't opening up at all and was still in lockdown mode. It made the outside world all the more perilous and I was very glad we were having this baby imminently and not in a month's time, around the original due date. It would have been so difficult to avoid getting Covid if it was being allowed to spread freely, and getting it would mean disaster.

Paul took the kids out for walks in the woods and my parents played games with them at home. I retreated, resting a lot and reading, in a feeble attempt to escape from my current reality and all that was bearing down on us.

God is our refuge and strength,
an ever-present help in trouble.
Therefore we will not fear, though the earth give way
and the mountains fall into the heart of the sea,
though its waters roar and foam
and the mountains quake with their surging.
(Psalm 46:1-3)

33
Birthdays

23rd February 2022

We faced a quandary for Paul's birthday: how do you celebrate a birthday with two preschoolers in the depth of winter when you're isolating? Especially when one of you can't stand for long or walk very far due to pelvic pain? It clearly had to be outdoors because we couldn't share breathing space with anyone potentially contaminated, and we were having all the time inside the house that we needed.

We were given inspiration and a financial gift by the charity called Zoe Faith,[33] whose website lists:

> MEMORIES IMPACT PROJECT
> Memories have the power to leave a lasting impact. Painful memories etch their way on to our hearts during difficult seasons. We want to make a way for joy-filled memories to co-exist in the grief and sorrow.
>
> We come alongside families who learn that their baby is not expected to live long past birth by providing them opportunities to make memories during their final months of pregnancy and offer support along the way.
>
> It might not be the same as imagined, but we believe that these memories will last a lifetime and leave a positive impact. We've witnessed that sprinkling joy and making memories along the way fosters hope and helps families feel supported.

---

[33] www.zoefaith.com/what-we-do#making memories (accessed 17th December 2024).

Inspired by the founder's story of embarking on trips and experiences to make memories after receiving a life-limiting diagnosis for their unborn child, we looked for activities nearby.

We settled on a local bird sanctuary, wrapped up warm and promised the kids a treat from the gift shop. They were fascinated by the owls and golden pheasants and loved seeing the penguins being fed, but soon got bored and didn't want to walk. Oh, the joys of being a toddler!

My parents went shopping in a nearby town that has a Lebanese restaurant and returned with a bag packed with fresh, flavourful Middle Eastern cuisine. What a treat! Ever since my time in the Middle East I have loved Lebanese food, and this felt like a great way to mark the day.

In the afternoon, Paul dropped me off at the hospital for my next round of checks and popped into town to buy some treats. The children were happy when we got home and they set up a game of shop downstairs. We didn't know this would be one of the last glimpses of normal family life for a while.

24th February 2022

I launched into full-on prep mode, getting every possible job done that I could think of, tidying every room and cleaning every nook and cranny in the house I could access. I knew we only had a few days left before the baby came, and I didn't want jobs outstanding. I wanted to be able to give my full attention to the baby and not be distracted at all.

Paul and I tried to discuss what the following week might look like, and found it impossible to plan. How could we work out a balance of the kids' needs with time with the baby, if we didn't know how much time the baby might have? Paul felt confident we'd make the right call when the decisions came up, and I prayed for God to guide us.

I wrote in my diary that evening:

> Three days to go. Very possibly my last three full days of ever being pregnant. Definitely hoping it's not the last three

days of this baby's life. Part of me is still hoping the diagnosis was a false positive and this baby is totally healthy.

25th February 2022 (morning)

... call on me in the day of trouble;
I will deliver you, and you will honour me.
(Psalm 50:15)

It was my father's birthday and there were still some jobs to finish.

We started the day with the children in our bed, cuddled up and reading stories together. Paul then gave them breakfast while I rested and prayed. I listened to 'Raise a Hallelujah' again and felt prompted to pray for those who would be praying for us. I felt I should pray they would have the faith for the baby to be born healthy and strong. In my mind, this was all for when the C-section was planned, in three days' time.

After breakfast, Paul took Jamie for a haircut while I labelled the colostrum in the freezer with my full name, date of birth and hospital number.

I also phoned Remember My Baby, a UK based charity whose 'mission is to offer professional, completely complimentary photography services to families navigating the profound loss of a baby'.[34]

I explained our situation and the expected time and place of birth and they made a note of it, asking us to confirm on Monday. Having professional photos of that morning and of us as a family together was something we wanted, to commemorate and celebrate a potentially short life.

Originally, I was supposed to have my final CTG that morning. I'd then been given an appointment for my pre-op for the afternoon and knew there was no way I'd go to the hospital twice or wait around for hours in between. When I'd called to move the pre-op for the C-section, they informed me it couldn't

---

[34] ww.remembermybaby.org.uk (accessed 21st January 2025).

be moved to the morning because the blood tests needed to be within seventy-two hours of the operation. So they offered to move the CTG later instead: a seemingly innocuous move that I will forever be grateful for.

We had a picnic lunch outside, enjoying some rare February sun, and I had a sudden thought that I had very few photos of the bump. I posed in the watery winter light, again not knowing this would capture my final moments of pregnancy.

As we ate outside, I registered I was feeling a slight sense of unease and tried to work out where it was coming from. It wasn't just a low level of nerves from the pre-op and CTG: I tended to find it fairly relaxing drifting along in the flow of hospital instructions and requests. Then it hit me. I hadn't felt the baby move as vigorously as before.

Mothers' intuition is a very real thing, and I believe can be trusted. It's often hard to put into words and explain what you're sensing, as your subconscious registers some change from the norm and alerts you to it before your conscious mind has a chance to catch up. It's when you notice everything has gone quiet and hunt down the kids to find them covered in food or art supplies. It's when you feel your child's skin or observe their behaviour, and you just know they're not well, even before obvious symptoms manifest. It's when you know your unborn baby's movements have changed, even if you can't describe how, or remember when you last felt movement.

This baby's movements had felt different from the previous two because they had grown so much bigger, and them having a lot less space to move around in caused me no little discomfort. This baby had always been so energetic, but now the actions felt less lively and spirited. I'm not sure it was enough of a worry that I would have phoned the helpline and asked for an appointment that day, but I was very glad I was being seen later that afternoon. As it turned out, I was right to be concerned.

34
Birth

After lunch I headed to the antenatal clinic in the hospital for my pre-op. It was conducted in the same room I'd had bloods taken after the initial consultant scan, and prompted me to reflect on the crazy journey we'd been on since then.

I had some time spare after the pre-op and before my final CTG, so I popped over to the coffee shop in the entrance of the hospital to join the eternally long queue and treat myself to a decaf flat white while I was hooked up to the monitors upstairs.

Still being too early for my next appointment, I decided to head upstairs to the maternity unit, in case a bed was free. I was ushered into the waiting room, casting a sympathetic glance at a very pregnant lady with her pacing husband and hospital bag, clearly waiting for an induction. It wasn't long before my name was called and I was back in a bay, tummy exposed and encircled by the coloured bands while we waited for the machine to bleep that everything was fine.

Drama was unfolding in the bay directly opposite me, and I was listening in and giving Paul a running commentary. A teenage girl was lying there, on her phone, with a young guy (presumably the father) leaning on the windowsill, also on his phone. It quickly became apparent there were some serious concerns about the baby's health, although neither parent seemed to register this. The baby had stopped growing at twenty-six weeks' gestation. The various health professionals coming in and out were trying to explain the mother needed to be moved to a more specialist hospital. This girl, however, didn't want to miss going to a party that evening and was negotiating a delayed transfer.

A midwife in a different-coloured uniform, who seemed skilled at talking with and persuading teenagers, tried her best to explain the danger to her baby of any delay, but the girl wasn't having any of it.

I sipped my coffee and shuffled into a more comfortable position on the bed and then glanced over at the output from the monitor. A baby's heart rate is shown as a continuous zigzag line on the top graph and should register within 110 and 160 beats per minute. I was alarmed to see it drop below those numbers but then it picked back up again and returned to normal. After the twelve minutes, the light on the machine turned to green and we were all good.

The midwife came over to have a look at the trace and, seeing the one deceleration, asked if I wouldn't mind staying on the machine a little longer, to make sure baby was alright. As I was enjoying this unfolding drama in front of me and any time away from the kids can feel like a break, I was happy to agree. I did mention the movements had felt a little less vigorous at lunchtime but that I hadn't been too concerned. I am so glad I stayed.

We waited out the hour and at one point I watched the line suddenly disappear and, after a pause that felt far too long, reappear again at ninety beats per minute. I felt fear unfurl in my chest. That didn't look good to me.

I took photos of the trace to send to Paul, focusing on the seriously concerning decelerations, and got a reply questioning the morality of sending over this poor girl's trace. Huh? I suddenly realised I'd gone seamlessly from updating him on the unfolding drama of the teenager in the bed opposite and sending him my trace.

'This isn't hers!' I messaged. 'How would I even get access to her printout? It's mine!'

The midwife had a quiet look at the trace and said she'd get hold of the doctor to come and have a chat with me.

The afternoon wore on as I stayed hooked up to the machine, and I noticed my phone battery was low as I'd been busy messaging.

'I don't want to come home', I wrote to Paul. 'I'm worried this baby won't last the weekend.' I had a sickening sense of returning on Monday only to find there was no heartbeat any more, or rushing in on Sunday after feeling no movement to discover the baby had already passed. We'd got this far and I was not going to risk anything now!

The doctor was a tall, young man and he asked if I understood what the trace meant. I said I wasn't medical but had had two children already and lots of CTGs, so I was guessing these heart decelerations were serious.

'Yes, it could mean the baby is in distress for some reason, or that the placenta isn't functioning as it should be. I see you're scheduled for a C-section on Monday morning. How do you feel about us getting the baby out now? As soon as we can?' he queried.

I almost burst into tears with relief. Anxiety had been building about the staff not listening to my fears and sending me home for the weekend, and I had been steeling myself for a fight, thinking I might need to apply pressure to get this baby out sooner. I was so glad we were on the same page, and quickly acquiesced.

'How soon can your partner get here? I assume he'll want to be present for the birth?'

'About half an hour. Could it really be that quick?' I was amazed.

'Well, tell him to come as soon as he can.'

I scanned through the notes on my phone to find the list of what was left to pack in the hospital bag, called Paul and told him to come as fast as possible, to add my hairbrush and deodorant to the hospital bag, to bring all the colostrum from the freezer and, oh yes, to pack my phone charger!

As soon as he arrived, I was walked from the antenatal ward through to the delivery suite and only then wondered what drama I'd provided for the other ladies in their bays, and how I would never know how it all played out with the teenager and her twenty-six-week pregnancy.

Now in a private room, we had forms to sign and new outfits to wear: Paul was clearly comfortable in his familiar scrubs and me rather uncomfortable in only a hospital gown. The decision was made to inject me with steroids for the baby's lung development, even if there wasn't enough time for it to fully take effect, and I had a Covid test then and there.

A paediatrician entered with my birth plan and talked through our desires for the birth, and I was grateful it was all written down and I didn't have to attempt to remember it in the heat of the moment. What we had neglected to add to the birth plan was a request for cord blood testing, and it never entered my head to ask for the placenta to be stored for genetic testing.

As I was walked from the room to the theatre, got seated on the bed and prepared for an epidural to numb me from the waist down, I remember noticing that I felt calm. I wondered, 'Am I feeling numb? Am I shutting down emotionally?' But no, it wasn't numb. It definitely was calm, almost peaceful. I wondered if it was because the moment of the big reveal was finally here. We had lived with the uncertainty for so long, and now we were about to find out quite how ill our baby was, or if they'd live a few hours or a few days – the wondering was coming to an end. I remembered how my friend with a young child with spina bifida had told me that once she'd been born, you got on with everything that needed to be done, whereas the not-knowing of pregnancy had felt a greater challenge.

Paul had messaged out to our WhatsApp prayer group that I was going for an emergency C-section after a concerning heart trace, and our pastor and his wife quickly arranged a prayer meeting over Zoom for 7pm. I'm sure the peace also flowed from being carried on their prayers.

While we waited for the epidural to take effect, we were asked if we'd like to play any music. I appreciated this, because I'd assumed a theatre birth would be drastically different from my previous births: very bright and clinical. I was grateful to be proved wrong as the lighting was lowered and our wishes for a peaceful environment were respected.

We tried to set my phone up with the Bluetooth speaker and I got flustered when it wouldn't connect and then needed to be charged. Paul wanted his phone to take photos and I couldn't find the song on my phone, so had to find an online version which kept stopping. I can remember wondering how such a small detail could matter so much to me! I guess I was concerning myself with an insignificant issue because I could do so little with anything that actually mattered. Eventually we got it sorted and the music swirled around us as I lay on my back and a drape was put across my chest to block the view of my lower body. Paul, seated by my head, held my hand and I looked up to see the time. It was exactly 7pm.

The cutting and tugging began and I wondered how long it would take before we knew how well our baby was. Five minutes later, I heard a noise: the cry we thought we might never hear. The drape was lowered and there before me was a teeny-tiny but wonderfully pink and loudly screaming baby!

'It's a girl!' someone announced.

Paul and I wept.

She looked incredibly healthy! It was beyond our wildest imagination. She needed no help breathing. There was no 'mewing' like a kitten or lack of a life force. This baby was vibrant and vigorous!

Paul took some photos and thankfully sent the one without my open abdomen and exposed internal organs to the prayer group. In the photo, Hope has her stick-thin left arm stretched out and her right hand curled towards her face as she cries heartily. Masked medical staff adorn the dark background as bloody gloved hands hold her up to the light.

Our GP friend, Steph, told us later that she'd been out for dinner for her dad's birthday and had burst into tears when she saw the photo, as she could recognise how well the baby looked, how full of life! Those who were praying on Zoom described it as the most memorable prayer meeting they'd ever attended, receiving a photo of a baby at the moment of birth, still shiny with blood.

Paul and I cried and cried as they lifted the drape again to stitch me back up and took the baby away to check her over and wrap her up. The paediatrician brought her round to me, quietly content in a white towel and yellow knitted hat, to say she had felt inside her mouth and not felt a cleft palate, and she had listened to her heart and not heard any murmur. We were stunned – had the specialist been wrong? Had she been healed? We were told she had an APGAR score of nine out of ten, which is where the baby's colour, heart rate, muscle tone and breathing are all checked.[35] She was, however, tiny, weighing 1.75 kilogrammes, or 3 pounds and 14 ounces, and therefore would need to be taken to SCBU. With lots of cuddles and photos done, we relinquished her to the Special Care nurses and poured out our amazement at how well she looked.

The paediatrician had said she couldn't rule out the presence of a genetic condition, so at this point we were marvelling that we were going to have a baby that lived. We also felt grateful for every person in the NHS who'd brought her safely into the world, and humbled at how all of this effort could be made for our family.

---

[35] APGAR stands for Appearance, Pulse, Grimace, Activity and Respiration and a score of seven to ten is considered healthy.

35
Aftermath

25th February 2025 (evening)

I was wheeled back to my private room, trying to find somewhere to plug in my phone to read all the lovely messages coming in from those on the WhatsApp group who'd seen the picture and were sharing our joy.

'I wasn't sure it was the right thing to do to send that photo,' Paul shared, 'but I was just so pleased!'

Paul went to visit Hope in SCBU and reported back that she was doing well and remarked excitedly on how adorable she was. I sat up in bed as we talked, slowly recovering the feeling in my legs, which were heavily wrapped in blankets. I suddenly felt a strange pouring sensation between my legs but decided not to mention it as I assumed it was something to do with the epidural wearing off.

Two midwives came in, thrilled to tell me they had been given permission to wheel me across to SCBU where I could see baby Hope in her incubator and put a hand in to touch her. I do remember noticing I didn't feel quite right, but no one checked in with me and I was desperate to see her again.

I was wheeled down the long corridor separating the maternity unit and SCBU, feeling excited and apprehensive. We were given new masks at the door, as was protocol, and soon shown into the Critical Care ward which only held Hope, lying prone in an incubator, with a tube out of her nose and wires attached to her chest and feet. Incredulous, I sat up to stretch my hand in through a hole to stroke her leg and suddenly felt distinctly unwell, very sick and dizzy.

At that point, I lost consciousness.

Paul reports he noticed I looked very pale and lay back with my eyes closed. One of the midwives tried to shrug it off as me being overcome by all the excitement of the day. Paul knew that wasn't it. The other midwife pulled the blankets off my lap to discover, with horror, around two litres of blood covering my legs.

I woke up some minutes later to immense pain. Pain that took my breath away.

I'd been wheeled in haste back to the room in the delivery suite and a doctor had been called, who started to massage my abdomen vigorously. She was putting huge pressure on my uterus to get it to start contracting to pass the clotting that was forming.

I had literally just been cut open and sown up below the area she was massaging and the pain was unbelievable. She kept apologising for it and quickly called for gas and air, explaining she needed to do this. I think Paul was mainly grateful I'd come round again!

Because of the bleed, I was placed in the High Dependency Unit and not allowed to visit Hope again that night. To be honest, I was in such ferocious agony that I was deeply grateful she was being taken care of by wonderfully experienced and compassionate nurses while I could focus on myself. I could not imagine trying to care for a baby, or attempting to do anything at all, in the state I was in!

A bed was pulled out for Paul, but he decided to head home and make sure everything was fine there after his rather hasty departure. I wish I'd had the forethought to ask him to stay. That night, I was simultaneously experiencing very contrasting feelings: I was incredibly grateful Hope was alive and seemingly well, and in the most acute physical pain I had ever endured. Labour pains can be overwhelmingly intense in the moment, but they rise and fall like waves and pass. This was constant and stunning in its intensity.

The midwife on duty came in with my dose of painkillers and there didn't seem to be very many. I'd learned after my first birth to take all the painkillers they give you and never refuse any because you feel OK in that moment! Oh, how quickly they can wear off.

I asked what the tablets were and I was being given one paracetamol and one ibuprofen as well as some morphine.

'One of each?' I questioned. 'Surely I should have two of each?'

'I'm sorry,' she explained sheepishly, 'but because your booking-in weight was below 50 kilogrammes, you're only allowed to have half of the normal dosage.'

With dismay, I realised they were using the weight I'd been at my first midwife appointment in the very early stages of pregnancy. I begged the midwife to change the dosage, explaining how I'd put on tons of weight during pregnancy, averaging two stone[36] with each previous one. She offered to check with the doctor and soon returned to deny me the full dosage, saying the doctor couldn't authorise it as she'd got into trouble recently doing exactly that.

I was tearful as I jokingly offered to get up off the bed to stand on scales right then and there. There was literally no way I could get off the bed, but it felt cruel to deny me the extra tablets when I was in so much pain. I didn't want to think about how I would have felt had Hope died.

SCBU has a special online communication tool set up for parents who can't remain with their baby, and I had a few unsuccessful attempts to connect, feeling bad asking the midwives to check again with SCBU if my request had come through. Eventually I was signed in and received a picture of Hope. My heart was full, even though my body was screaming.

I couldn't sleep at all so played a track on my phone that Paul and I had recorded for the birth of our first daughter. It was Paul reading encouraging verses from Psalms and Isaiah in a

---

[36] 12 kilogrammes or 28 pounds.

soothing voice over relaxing music. I had two ten-minute recordings and I listened over and over, trying to find solace for my soul while my body was in torment.

One of my closest long-term friends, Georgina, was awake late into the night, and we messaged back and forth for a long while. Talk about being there for a friend exactly in their moment of need!

That was a night I hope to never repeat and, to date, goes down as my worst night ever physically, even though emotionally I was riding on a high from Hope being born alive and looking so well. I felt a strong compassion for those who endure a C-section and its aftermath, with no baby to hold or care for afterwards. I, however, felt so lucky I'd get to see my baby again in the morning… if the morning ever came!

36
Hospital: Day one

26th February 2022

> You desired faithfulness even in the womb;
> you taught me wisdom in that secret place.
> (Psalm 51:6)

Having a baby in SCBU was a powerful motivator to get out of bed and start moving the next morning. A number of people helped me sit up, swivel and then be transferred to a wheelchair to head over to see Hope again. My tiny, living miracle!

A cute, colourful sign had been put up in her bay, listing her name, date of and weight at birth, our names as her parents and her named consultant. We were pleased to meet this gentle paediatrician, Dr Grant, and although he confirmed she didn't seem to have the full version of Edwards' syndrome, he was reserved about her situation and brought us back down to earth. He suggested she might have a partial or mosaic form of the condition, or maybe even another genetic condition entirely. He told us we couldn't rule anything out at this stage and didn't want us to get our hopes up until we knew for sure what was going on.

It felt like pretty big news and we were told she would have blood tests in two days' time, at the start of the week, and the earliest we'd hear would be the end of the following week. While we were still overjoyed Hope was very much alive, the consultant's opinion had been sobering.

I was returned to a different room on the delivery suite and manoeuvred from wheelchair to bed with great difficulty. I was grateful we weren't aiming for me to be discharged after twenty-four hours to travel to the hospice, as I felt barely able to move!

One of the older and very experienced SCBU nurses, Anna, conspired with the midwife assigned to me to reunite Hope and me. She was incredible and brought Hope to me! Because SCBU was unusually quiet that day, she wheeled her little incubator over to my room and was set on us having time to bond. Hope was jaundiced and needed to be under a bright light, but knowing the value of having skin-to-skin time, she gave me Hope to cuddle, careful to position all the wires and tubes in safe places, and lay a portable phototherapy device next to her skin, under blankets. It felt so right and fitting to have her so close. After a baby has been in your womb for nine months, physically encased in your body, having them apart from you is unnerving, like you've suddenly lost a limb. The world felt put to rights when we were touching, even if the future for her remained very unknown. I knew we'd face it together.

Another paediatrician came in on his day off to conduct a scan of Hope's heart, to check if there was anything of concern. Thankfully she remained asleep as he spent a while checking for pulmonary stenosis or holes in the heart and he chatted with us while we waited for his report. It turned out he was Egyptian and from Heliopolis, an area of Cairo that I'd lived in before getting married. I explained how I'd arrived just before the revolution of January 2011 and the Arab Spring and how I'd loved living in Egypt so much I stayed for five years.

When the scan was complete, he could tell us he'd not seen any evidence of anything concerning, except for two small holes that should close up by themselves in the fulness of time. One was expected to close up within a few days and the other within six months. We were pleased and amazed, asking ourselves again whether the specialist had misdiagnosed an issue with her heart, or if Hope had been healed as we'd prayed. Either way, it was wonderful news and we determined not to worry about the small holes if the specialists weren't.

'Her heart has very good function,' he was pleased to tell us, informing us she'd have another scan after a week. Then he returned to his own family, to enjoy their weekend activities. Time after time, NHS staff went out of their way to care for us, and we'll never forget it.

When it came to Hope's next feed, Anna had plans. Hope had been fed all of the colostrum I'd provided and was now on formula. While I do support breastfeeding, I am also hugely grateful for formula when it doesn't work out quite as expected or hoped. Anna suggested I try feeding Hope myself, directly from the breast. This was a totally new idea as we'd been resigned to her being unable to breastfeed and potentially tube-fed her whole life – it hadn't occurred to us she would ever feed by herself.

Getting any newborn to latch on can be tricky and is one of the main causes of stress in those first few days and weeks, but with the right (and regular) support, once breastfeeding is established, I had found it does get easier. Anna did a valiant job trying to get Hope to feed, and even managed to get her to latch on twice and suck a little bit. Tiny Hope quickly tired, though, and was given a full feed through her NG tube.

In the afternoon, Paul headed home to spend time with the children, and my mother came to be with me. I napped as Hope was returned to SCBU and then was told it was time for me to attempt to walk to the bathroom. I didn't feel ready for this, but they kept reassuring me that the best recovery was an active one and the sooner I got up and walked, the sooner I'd be walking around more comfortably. Trying to be a pliant patient, I agreed, and with much help (and protestations of pain), I did make it to the bathroom and was even dressed back in my own clothes (a very loose maternity nightie that might have resembled a tent), glad to finally get out of the hospital gown.

Paul returned once Martha and Jamie were down for the night, and supported me walking to SCBU to spend the evening with Hope. Still jaundiced and unable to retain body warmth, she remained in an incubator under a bright light, with her eyes covered in protective patches. We chatted and processed all that had happened, and he told me cards and gifts were already starting to arrive.

He headed home after escorting me safely back to my room, and I wrote up the last two very eventful days in my diary.

Near 11pm, a knock on the door pre-empted a midwife that I assumed was coming in to take observations like blood pressure and temperature. That wasn't all she had to say.

'I'm so sorry but we need this room for someone in labour as it's really busy, and we need to transfer you to the postnatal ward. Don't worry, you will still have a private room as it's hard when you don't have your baby with you, but would it be OK to move now?'

I still needed help getting up, and she carried all the belongings and snacks I couldn't, and I soon settled down to sleep in a slightly smaller room further down the corridor but behind the doors separating delivery from postnatal. Foremost in my mind as I nodded off was my desire to see Martha and Jamie somehow the next day.

37
Hospital: Week one

27th February 2022

> For what you have done I will always praise you
> in the presence of your faithful people.
> And I will hope in your name,
> for your name is good.
> (Psalm 52:9)

Hospitals on a Sunday have a very different feel – the busyness and noise of weekday outpatient appointments are replaced by the quiet and stillness of empty corridors.

Paul came to sit with me in Hope's bay in SCBU and we continued debriefing and processing together. He shared with me how, as he'd considered the challenges of having a dependent disabled child, he'd found this verse kept coming to mind: 'hope does not disappoint' (Romans 5:5, NKJV). God was giving him a framework for our future: no matter what the genetic results came back to say, Hope would not disappoint us. He continued to say our focus is our family and that would continue, even if it looked different from what we'd expected. I was grateful he'd come to a place of peace, and I was finding myself on a similar journey. I was no longer questioning if I'd somehow caused this by starting to try for a baby too early and I was coming to see Hope as the gift from God that she is.

'He created her and loves her and she is exactly who she was always meant to be', I wrote in my diary that day.

Paul headed home at lunchtime and returned in the afternoon with the children, which was such a joy. They sat on a bench outside with my mother, all wrapped up from the cold, while Paul found a wheelchair and brought me all the way downstairs and outside – definitely further than I felt able to walk at that point. Jamie gave me the biggest, cutest smile when he saw me, and I cuddled up with them on the bench to hear their news and answer their questions. They seemed totally fine with my sudden disappearance, and I felt deeply grateful for secure and resilient kids. I came to understand they'd barely register this absence in the course of their lives as I'd been continuously present up to this point and I would be again sometime soon, so this little blip was just that: an aberration soon forgotten. It wouldn't be long before they'd take my unceasing presence for granted again.

After a while, they were restless, so my parents took them home while Paul wheeled me back up to my room. He set off home in time for their tea and I got set up with a noisy, hospital-grade, electric double-breast pump. The midwife who showed me how to use the machine had advised me to relax and recline on the bed while I pumped, which I did, only to find myself absolutely stuck. I had no tummy muscles to pull myself upright and my two hands were taken up with holding the pumps and attached milk storage bottles! There was no flat surface close enough to put one of the bottles down, and I couldn't even reach the machine to turn it off, or the alarm to call for help! Eventually I found a way to balance one bottle on my legs and then push myself far enough up on one elbow to reach a table. Never again did I recline to pump or sit too far from a cleared surface area!

I managed to pump about twenty millilitres in two attempts, which made up one full feed for Hope. She was being fed every two hours and the amount she needed daily was worked out according to her weight. By the time Paul had returned in the evening, she'd been changed to feeds every three hours and so the amount per feed had been increased to twenty-six millilitres, the first of which she promptly vomited down my front. This was all normal behaviour for a newborn baby and I wasn't fazed.

These were the ordinary moments I'd thought I might miss and held a sweetness, even if it was also rather sticky!

That evening, I was in the bed in my private room and fast asleep by 10pm.

28th February 2022

I woke up at 1.30am and thought it as good a time as any to express more milk. Newborns feed incessantly, and knowing feeding overnight is important for establishing a mother's milk supply, I went with it. I knew Hope was feeding at 2am so I hobbled over to SCBU, smiling wanly at the midwife on duty in the postnatal ward as I passed, curious as to what she thought of me – admiring my dedication to express, pitying me for having a baby in SCBU or thinking me foolish for relinquishing sleep? Who knows.

After her feed, I sat and held Hope for an hour in the darkened, quiet ward and then returned to bed. It was a precious moment.

When Paul arrived later, we met a specialist nurse who'd checked Hope over and had more sobering news to share with us. In her opinion, Hope was starting to display some markers for Edwards', like overlapping fingers, low-set ears and pouches under the eyes. After thoroughly looking her over, she'd noticed a wrinkle or dimple at the bottom of her spine and reported she had a floppy core and a head lag, even though her limbs had good muscle tone. She informed us Hope had had a twenty-second apnoea, where she'd stopped breathing, and this chilled us. This is how we'd been told babies with Edwards' die, when their apnoeas increase in duration and frequency until they no longer breathe again.

Suddenly, it seemed like our initial euphoria was tragically misplaced. Maybe she did have the full form of the genetic condition, and maybe our time with her was limited. As I cuddled her that afternoon, I gazed into her face and wondered if she could see or hear anything. There was no way to know in this early stage, and we had to wait until it all became clear.

Results coming at the end of the week now seemed a long way off.

Another issue was that she didn't seem to have a consistent gag reflex, so she would have to continue being tube-fed as we were told it wasn't safe to attempt bottle or breastfeeding. This felt like a step backwards and was sorely disappointing.

This had been the day of the planned C-section, the day we thought we'd be welcoming her into the world, and now those extra few days felt like a gift. More special time for us to spend with her while she lived. My parents came in that afternoon and were able to hold her, after following the ward's hygiene protocols. The photos we took were bittersweet as we wondered how many we'd have with her.

That wasn't the only drama to unfold that day, unfortunately.

Paul told me later how he'd heard a strange noise that afternoon emanating from behind the dishwasher. He soon established there was a leak and tried to find a plumber to come and sort it out. The plumber found a lead water pipe that had deteriorated and caused the leak, but when he tried to turn the water off at the mains, he couldn't as the stop tap was stuck and wouldn't budge. It all sounded very stressful, as they then had to call out the water board, who dug up part of the pavement outside our house! The upshot was that our house was left with no water supply and we needed to find another plumber who was free to fix it all. As if we needed any more drama and stress in our lives!

Late in the evening, Paul returned to the hospital just as I'd been ousted from my room again. There had been a lot of ladies having a lot of babies, and I was to be discharged from postnatal care to free up the room. The midwife offered to set up a camp bed for me in Hope's bay as they weren't sure I would be able to get in and out of the chairs that convert into beds in SCBU. I was given a bag of medication and a box of syringes to inject myself with and took up my next residence, alongside Hope's cot in SCBU. At least I would be close to her and able to express milk for each feed, I thought.

1st March 2022

> Surely God is my help;
> the Lord is the one who sustains me.
> (Psalm 54:4)

I was able to pop home in the afternoon, and Martha and Jamie were very confused.

'Where is the baby?' Jamie asked, looking at my bulge of a tummy that could easily have still held a newborn.

'Can the baby stay at the hospital and you come home now?' Martha looked hopeful.

The day had felt rather intense, mainly because of the lack of water at home. My father had been filling buckets of water from our next-door neighbour's outdoor tap so they could flush the toilet cisterns and wash hands.

Our church community started a meal rota for us that very day, and the first family who delivered food also gave us disposable plates and cutlery so we didn't even have to wash up! It was very considerate. Those who could not cook for us donated money to help cover the costs of parking and buying lunch at the hospital and other expenses that came up.

Paul's parents arrived, as we'd arranged for them to visit the day after Hope was supposed to be born – the plan being we'd be at the hospice by then. Instead, they were at a house with no water and only able to pop in briefly to visit the baby in hospital.

I was grateful I could shower in SCBU and had spent the morning busy with my routine of expressing every three hours to match Hope's feeds, and learning how to feed her though the NG tube.

Now Hope was a few days old, it was time for another heart scan, conducted using a mobile scanning unit in SCBU, and we were glad to hear that one of the holes was no longer visible and there was only a small ASD[37] present.

---

[37] An atrial septal defect is a hole between the upper chambers of the heart.

Awkwardly for me, my ankles puffed up, which is normal after a C-section but made finding footwear to return home in very difficult. I ended up wearing flip-flops even though it was wet and wintry weather. Other friends offered lifts from hospital to home and back again, as I wasn't able to drive after the C-section and there was a lot going on at home for Paul to be occupied with!

As the days went by and I became more settled in the SCBU routine, we started to find a daily rhythm, which included Paul being present for the doctor's round mid-morning and me being home in time for the children's evening routine.

The nurses suggested I spend a night at home to get a full night of sleep, where I wouldn't be interrupted by all the bleeps and alarms going off. At this point, we still didn't know how much time we'd have with Hope, so I said I couldn't risk losing a night with her. Also, whenever I was away, she seemed to have her most unsettled times and I wanted to be there to hold her if she needed me. We remained incredulous she was here with us and doing so well.

2nd March 2022

Hope had an unsettled morning. I'd had a coffee the day before, as I find caffeine an effective laxative, which the painkillers had given me need for. I put her agitation and inability to sleep down to the presence of caffeine in the expressed milk she'd had, so I vowed to stick to decaf in the future! I ended up cradling her in my arms from 3.30am, planning to snatch an extra hour of sleep later. I knew I was having the newborn week fairly easy as the nurses were doing most of the night feeds, so I wasn't awake overnight as much as I had been after my previous births.

The doctor on the round that morning said more bloods needed to be taken from Hope, and he started the difficult job of teasing blood out of the tiny veins in her left hand. When this had happened before, the specialist nurse had given Hope sucrose to calm her, which had worked well. Not this time! She screamed and writhed and seemed in agony as I tried to hold her other hand and whisper soothing words to her. It was a distressing experience and I was left quite shaken.

As Hope and I recovered from this ordeal, there were suddenly shouts and cries from the ward next door. I could hear someone shout the doctor's first name and then all the staff rushed in that direction. I wondered what was happening and prayed urgently for any baby in that Critical Care ward to live. I felt tears prick my eyes as I looked down at Hope and felt desperately grateful it wasn't her.

Our ward door was closed by a member of staff and I noticed I was the only adult left present. A lot of concerned-looking people were coming and going in the corridor outside, and then, all of a sudden, Hope's oxygen monitor started to go off, signalling an apnoea. I looked down at her and saw she was breathing normally, her chest was rising and falling and she remained pink. 'Huh,' I thought to myself. 'What if her previous apnoea wasn't a real one either, and just the monitor dislodging? Also, what if another baby's alarms started to sound for real and I wasn't here? Would anyone know?'

Eventually a nurse came through to tell me one of the student nurses had collapsed, and when a crash team had been called to 'Adult; SCBU', they assumed it was a mistake and didn't attend straight away. My shoulders relaxed and I could feel tension dissipate on hearing it hadn't been a baby in crisis.

Paul came at lunchtime and I told him about the collapse and the doctor taking bloods and he said I could have requested him to stop, and to make sure sucrose is available next time. 'How would a non-medical parent know that?' I wondered.

While he was there, I lay on my camp bed to have a rest and a lady came round to speak with us. During the day, I kept the curtain around the bay open, as there were always health professionals coming and going, unless I was expressing milk and wanted some privacy. This lady was someone who wasn't dressed in hospital clothes and she introduced herself as a therapist. She explained that parents who find themselves in SCBU can be in shock and find their new reality hard to deal with, so she was employed to have informal chats and help them process.

We filled her in on how we'd found ourselves there, and how we were actually grateful to still be there and not at the hospice as Hope was doing well. We told her how we were waiting on genetic testing and were trying to prepare ourselves for potentially having a living child with a disability.

She helped frame how we'd been through massive shifts in our understanding of what our family was going to look like: having a third child, not having a third child, then on to having a disabled third child for who knew how long? Another thing she was able to shed light on was my sleep. I don't remember how we got on to this, but I'd mentioned I was sleeping extremely deeply in Hope's bay in SCBU, even with the noise of alarms going off and members of staff moving around and coming into the bay to feed Hope. One night I'd set an alarm on my phone to wake up to express and help with Hope's feed and one of the nurses kindly turned it off after a while of me sleeping through it.

'I wonder if you're able to rest more deeply now because you know she's close to you and is safe and well taken care of. Some of the uncertainty is gone?'

It was true. I'd slept badly for so many months, not only because of being pregnant but also because of the worry and concern for Hope. Now she was in the safest place she could be, and I could trust that others would run to her aid should anything happen. She was safe and I could rest.

By the evening, the water at home had been restored after a plumber had worked on it almost all day, and the children had found it more normal for me to pop back again for a short period of time. I was hoping home life would be a bit easier now as I settled back down in my camp bed for another night in SCBU. I had learned the hard way that if I lay flat on my back I couldn't get up again; there were no handholds or a remote control to tip the bed up, and I couldn't shift on to my side to push myself up with one hand. There are no alarms if you're not the patient and not always a nurse nearby to help yank you up, so I had to be careful how I lay down or I ended up like a beetle stranded on its back with its legs flailing around, frantic and fruitless. Having a C-section had repercussions I hadn't been expecting!

38
The geneticist

3rd March 2022

> As for me, I call to God,
> and the LORD saves me …
> He rescues me unharmed
> from the battle waged against me …
> (Psalm 55:16, 18a)

Our world was about to change once again. Unable to eat in the wards for hygiene reasons, I was sat in the kitchen in SCBU, tucking into a plate of leftovers from yesterday's delivered dinner, when Hope's consultant, Dr Grant, came to find me.

'We've got the first set of results back. Would you like to come to Hope's bay?'

I immediately abandoned my plate, hooked my face mask back over my ears and nose, and walked as fast as felt appropriate down the corridor.

I sat next to Paul, casting him a glance of concern and taking his hand. We thought at this point Hope could potentially still have full Edwards' but that she somehow might have a less severe presentation of the condition.

I held my breath as Dr Grant told us the news: 'The initial genetic testing shows that Hope does *not* have the full form of Trisomy 18.'

He paused to let the news sink in as Paul and I sat, astonished and speechless. He was such a kind and gentle man, I was glad he was able to give us the news. I exhaled slowly, almost unable to take in this new twist after all we'd been through.

'She could have a partial or mosaic form,' he continued, 'or another genetic condition, or there could have been something wrong with the placenta. The full results from the genetic testing and the testing on the placenta won't come back for another week or two. So we still don't know what we're dealing with, but this is very good news.'

The world in front of us suddenly opened up. Our whole future as a family shifted again. No longer were we contemplating a life expectancy for our baby being numbered in weeks or months, but years or even decades! It was a hugely emotional moment. The story of our family of five now extended ahead of us, full of happy memories and normal family experiences, and we were in shock.

'A geneticist has a satellite clinic here tomorrow. She's had a cancellation mid-morning and is able to fit you in.'

We marvelled at the incredible timing – the next day we were able to talk with an expert who had experience of babies with genetic conditions, and she might be able to explain fully what all of this might mean for Hope and for us.

This was such big news.

Hope does not have the full form of Trisomy 18. She does not have full Edwards' syndrome. We struggled to take it in.

But what did partial or mosaic mean again? I wanted to launch into all the research that existed to find out. I was in awe as I wrote in my diary that evening:

She could have a rare form of an extremely rare disease. Who could have expected this? What if it's not even T18 but something rarer *or* only something wrong with the placenta, meaning she might not have anything wrong at all? Not going to dwell on these questions but thank and worship God. What a journey this has been for us, and it is far from over yet.

4th March 2022

When I am afraid, I put my trust in you …
For you have delivered [Hope] from death …
that [she] may walk before God
in the light of life.
(Psalm 56:3, 13)

Paul drove into the hospital early, and we waited together to see the geneticist. The staff in SCBU wheeled Hope into the empty ward next door, set up chairs for us and closed the door, delicately giving us privacy. I'd been so used to having all of our conversations overheard by any other parents present or the staff bustling around that I found the environment a bit unsettling.

The geneticist walked into the ward and shook our hands. After completing all the newborn checks that every doctor who'd seen her so far had already done, the geneticist explained they'd read all of our notes and drew us a diagram on paper as they talked. The explanation started with the very basics of how an egg and sperm come together to form an embryo and explained how, as cells divide and multiply, a genetic condition can develop when every single cell has an extra copy of a certain chromosome. For Edwards' syndrome, it's the eighteenth chromosome, hence being called Trisomy 18.

We nodded along, this being within our remit of knowledge.

Here is where things got interesting: 'Sometimes,' the geneticist continued, 'only a certain cell line develops the mutation, but not the other lines, which is called mosaicism. So some of the baby's cells are affected but not all. It is possible for this mutation to reverse as the cells continue to multiply, so it could mean, for example, a certain organ might be affected but nothing else in the body.

'It is possible for only the placenta to contain the mutation and not the baby herself. In this case, the extra chromosomes are confined to the placenta and the baby is not affected at all.

194

It is called "confined placental mosaicism" [CPM], and this is what I think might have happened in your case.

'The NIPT test picks up placental cells in the mother's bloodstream and not foetal cells, so it is effectively checking the genetic code of the placenta. We know for sure there were placental cells in your NIPT test that had Trisomy 18. It should have been explained to you that it was only indicating that and that further testing, such as an amniocentesis, would tell us for sure if your baby had it too.

'From looking Hope over, I think her appearance is consistent with a baby who has been born very early or very small. Babies with genetic conditions tend to be in proportion as they are small all over, but Hope has a much larger head in comparison to her body. This is often the case with placental deficiency, as the head will develop first because of the importance of the brain. Any physical characteristics that might appear abnormal could be due to her small size and, I'd expect will all become typical in appearance over time.'

Again, the world was shifting beneath our feet and we felt humbled at this incredible news. This person who had held Hope so tenderly and carefully was fast becoming some kind of magical figure to us, like a fairy godmother who had swooped into the story to deliver stunningly good news and change the whole course of our narrative.

My diary that evening was bursting with emotion and praise:

> So Hope might not even have partial or mosaic T18. She could be a totally normal baby who was tiny due to placental deficiency. Oh Lord, how majestic is Your name in all the earth. You heard my cries for mercy. You told me to pray for life and strength and You gave it. You are good. You walked with us through the fire and we were not burned. We didn't even know it was possible to have a genetic condition confined to the placenta, so we never prayed for that![38]

---

[38] Scriptures in this diary entry from Psalm 8:1; Isaiah 43:2.

I wrote an update for social media and for our WhatsApp group and was flooded with messages of praise and thanksgiving and support. I had a sense that just as God 'set all the boundaries of the earth' (Psalm 74:17), so did He set the boundaries of exactly how far this genetic condition could advance: the placenta and no further. Hope was our little miracle, and our response was praise!

39
Hospital: Week two

5th March 2022

We had a surprise but welcome visit this morning from the paediatrician who'd been present at Hope's birth.

'I'm so sorry for not coming any earlier but I've not been working this past week, so this is the first chance I've had,' she explained.

She wanted to debrief the birth, explaining how she'd carefully read through the birth plan but then decided it couldn't be followed when such a healthy-looking baby emerged. She wanted to know what the geneticist had to say, and I wondered if Hope might become well known in the hospital paediatric unit as the Edwards' baby who didn't have Edwards'!

We'd started to receive questions from friends and family as to whether we thought Hope had been miraculously healed from T18 or if there had been a misdiagnosis. How could we answer that? We'll never know for sure, though I remembered how I'd not felt led to pray for healing, but for life, and so maybe Hope had never actually needed healing, but she definitely had needed prayer for life with a failing placenta! I was desperately hoping for the testing on it to come back to confirm CPM so that we could know for sure that she didn't have any level of it in her body.

I was also starting to feel the pull to return home. The first week in hospital had been one of survival, of not knowing what we were facing, but now I was starting to feel torn between my children. I was having long stretches of the day apart from Martha and Jamie, but then when I was home, Hope was left alone. She'd been relaxed and sleepy all day until I headed back, but when I returned later, the timings of her feeds were out and she'd been put to lie on her tummy. Newborns are always advised to sleep on their back as research has shown it reduces the chances of cot death, so I was confused to find her in this position.

'She got very unsettled after you left,' a nurse was able to tell me. 'We had to bring her feed forward as she seemed hungry, and then we found she seemed more comfortable on her front. It's safe to do that here because we're monitoring her so closely.'

I found it hard to think she'd been upset and I'd not been there to comfort her. Yet I did have to go home and see my other kids too. It felt a real stretch with no perfect way to keep the balance.

Originally, Dr Grant had wanted to keep Hope in until we got all the results back and therefore knew what or if anything was wrong. Also, babies were supposed to weigh 1.8 kilogrammes before they could be discharged from SCBU and Hope, as is normal with newborns, had lost some weight following birth and was still to regain her birth weight of 1.75 kilogrammes. It felt like we still had a bit of a mountain to climb before we could get her home.

As I cuddled her asleep, singing my songs of love to and over her, I shed a few more tears as the reality sank down into my heart that she was coming home and that we would get to see her grow up. Emotionally, I felt this whole journey had been overwhelming, and I wasn't sure how we'd even start to process it all. My desire to get her home was also fuelled by the ward on SBCU getting busier and noisier as more babies were admitted and more mothers stayed overnight.

Sunday was weighing day. Babies in SCBU were weighed twice a week and I was hoping she'd have gained enough weight to give us a glimmer of hope of returning home.

The scales said 1.7 kilogrammes or 3 pounds and 12 ounces: still under her birth weight and a fair way off the necessary weight to be discharged. It was hard not to feel a little discouraged and impatient.

When the paediatrician for that week came round, we expressed our desire to get her home, knowing now there might be nothing wrong with her. She wasn't on any medication and we'd both been trained how to feed her through an NG tube.

'We'll have to wait until she has a SALT assessment first,' she told us.[39] The speech and language team were going to verify the lack of a gag reflex and advise whether oral feeding might be safe to try. If she couldn't gag, then the risk of choking on milk would be too high for her to be bottle fed.

'If it's unsafe to feed orally, with a bottle or breastfeeding, then you'll be able to go home either Tuesday or Wednesday as you'll just be continuing to feed as you are now. If the assessment shows it is safe for her to attempt breastfeeding, then they probably will want you to stay in at least till the end of the week so you can get the support you need.'

Again, I felt torn. I knew breastfeeding would be best for her, but another week of sleeping on a camp bed in a busy ward, living out of a tiny case, apart from my older children, seemed a substantial sacrifice. I prayed a prayer of submission, asking for God's will to be done. I wanted to go home but I also wanted her to breastfeed. 'Lord, have Your way,' I whispered in my heart.

Rowena drove me home that afternoon, saying she'd wanted to see me and find out in person how I was doing. She also had something to tell me: 'In church on Sunday we were singing "Raise a Hallelujah", the song we'd sung when we'd first heard Hope might not live. I was struck by the line about hope arising from ashes – is that what prompted you to call her Hope?'

I'd not noticed that before! Or maybe it hadn't taken on the meaning that it did right now. I remembered the day of Hope's birth when, watching that song and Jonathan Helser's testimony, I'd felt prompted to pray for an increase of faith for

---

[39] SALT stands for 'speech and language therapy'.

those praying for the baby. It felt gratifying for this song to feature again, with one of its lines speaking clearly to us. Hope had indeed risen up!

A less enjoyable part of the day was realising I had developed mastitis. Pumping removes the milk less effectively than a tiny hungry mouth and now I had redness, pain and swelling and needed a course of antibiotics. This wasn't the first time I'd had it and I knew what to do, but now I had the added difficulty of timing my meals around the pills as well as the SCBU routine.

Also, Jamie had developed a heavy cold. We did not want this to be passed on to Hope, so our handwashing before entering her bay or before picking her up became even more elaborate; suddenly, the idea of taking her home into a potentially infectious environment seemed less attractive. Any newborn can suffer badly with a common cold because their nostrils are minuscule and easily blocked and they need to be able to breathe through them to feed. Hope's nose was even smaller and we didn't want her body fighting an infection. We were told she was using the calories consumed to keep warm because her body was so little and we needed her to put on weight, not use her remaining energy battling germs.

7th March 2022

I had been lulled into a sense of stillness and quiet over the weekend at the hospital and was not prepared for the barrage of visitors we were to receive on Monday morning. I was grateful I was up and dressed before 7.30am, when two male doctors I'd not seen before rushed in to attend to a baby across from Hope's bay. The other babies looked like dolls when they were picked up and moved around, and this one had got an infection and was struggling to breathe. I hoped and prayed all would be OK, and soon the intensity died down and life on the ward returned to normal.

The first of our visitors was Sarah, the specialist nurse who, on her ward round, surprised us by asking if we'd like to be discharged today or tomorrow. This was a different timeframe than we'd been led to expect!

Then the paediatric physiotherapist, who happened to be a friend from church, came to show us some exercises to do with Hope to help strengthen her core and neck muscles. She explained their department liked to be proactive and introduce interventions before problems occurred so they never did, rather than only responding once there were clear issues. Paul made a joke about, 'Who ever does the exercises a physio sets anyway?' which was met with a roll of the eyes and a wry smile.

Following her was a lady from the speech and language team to assess Hope and give us a plan to work up slowly to oral feeding. Unfortunately, Hope was deeply asleep when she came round and not at all interested in feeding, so we didn't get a clear indication of her abilities or potential difficulties. We were advised to dip her dummy in breast milk so she'd get a taste for it and associate food with her mouth and with flavour. This didn't seem like much forward progress, which was disappointing, and I assumed we'd continue with the NG tube.

A dietician followed closely behind to get our details and to reassure us that all the equipment we would need for tube-feeding would be given to us, and the community nurses would be our point of contact once we were home.

Then the hearing screening lady came round with her trolley of equipment as I joked with Paul I'd never get a chance to express Hope's next feed or get to the kitchen and eat breakfast! I was used to one of the hearing screening tests as my other two had received it, but she informed me babies who'd had an extended stay in hospital needed another one before they could be discharged. It was all rather a palaver with wheeling Hope's cot into a quiet private bay where she could be hooked up with lots of wires and contraptions. She needed to stay still for a certain length of time and it was a relief when she passed straight away and we were given the all-clear from that team. It was so reassuring to know there were no issues with her hearing!

Our final visitor that morning was the therapist who'd seen us before. She was in tears as we explained what we'd learned from the geneticist and how it looked like Hope would be totally fine.

I was exhausted by the time I'd popped home to see the kids, eaten, helped put them to bed and then returned. I was also deeply appreciative for our church community who'd provided meals and lifts. Our community were carrying us and removing the potential stress of the practical aspects of having a family split between a house and a hospital.

As I got back to my makeshift home from home, I started to express milk when Hope began to get a bit fractious. I still had to finish pumping, wash and sterilise the equipment, put leftovers in the fridge for tomorrow's lunch, give myself the last injection, take that evening's (full) dose of painkillers, brush my teeth and get changed for bed. A nurse kindly cuddled Hope while I did all those as quickly as I could, then I settled into my chair with Hope in one arm and wrote my diary with the other, feeling impressed with myself for managing to do it with the book perched on the armrest. It wasn't until later that I saw how scrawly and scraggly the writing looked! Ah well, it was another day until home, where I'd be able to carry her around while doing all the tasks I needed to there.

8th March 2022

I spent all my time at home in the afternoon getting everything ready for Hope's arrival. The Moses basket was set up downstairs in the lounge and the next-to-me crib in our bedroom; the baby car seat was placed in the car with the newborn insert inside, as well as the freezer bag for all the extra milk I'd pumped. I laid out the tiny sleeping bags and baby blankets ready, and put the electric double pump on to charge. We were going to bring our baby home! It was time for her to meet her sister and brother.

I was praying nothing would happen to stop her getting home, and I had to do a whole night of feeds myself to show the staff we were able to adequately take care of her. That involved waking every three hours to warm her milk, test the NG tube was in her tummy and not her lungs by extracting some liquid and testing its acidity levels, and then pour the milk into the new syringe attached to her tube and wait for gravity to pull it all into her tummy. It actually took a lot less time than breast or bottle feeding!

Paul was taught how to reinsert an NG tube on a specially designed doll in case Hope's became dislodged, and I was given the safe sleep talk. Being discharged from SCBU with a baby was a very thorough process compared to taking a baby home from the postnatal ward. We were given one hundred syringes to take home for feeds, and we took and sent a video to the SALT team of Hope successfully completing her dummy dips. She clearly enjoyed sucking the milk on the dummy and had no issues with the suck–breathe–swallow action.

As we prepared to leave, I became aware of how much I'd miss all the staff there. The nurses had been absolutely fantastic. They were so friendly and chatty, graciously showing us how to care for Hope in this unfamiliar environment and journeying with us through the emotional ups and downs since her birth. I wasn't sure we could ever thank them enough.

9th March 2022

This morning was all systems go to get Hope home!

Paul arrived first thing in the morning, and we both had to do resuscitation training and settle Hope safely into her car seat. She was too small, even with the newborn insert, so a nurse showed us how to roll up a blanket to put under her bottom to support her and ensure the straps were across the right parts of her body. With the discharge checklist done, we were asked for the parking permit back and I looked blank.

'You weren't given a parking permit during your induction here?'

'My what?'

It turns out I'd missed an induction in my late-night camp bed transfer and we'd ended up paying for two weeks of parking at the hospital when it should have been free. Now I understood why it had taken a few days to be told I could have a complimentary breakfast after every night I slept there. It made me feel even more grateful we'd been kindly given money to cover these costs!

Anyway, nothing could dampen our joy as we stood by the entrance for our obligatory 'leaving SCBU' photograph. Paul and I raised our hands in triumph and celebration as we carried Hope in the car seat between us, full of amazement and gratitude that we were bringing this living, breathing, tiny baby home to where she belonged.

40
Home

March 2022

The full emotional fallout of what we'd been facing didn't start to hit me until we were home. Friends popped round with cards and gifts, tears in their eyes as they held Hope and marvelled with us at how tiny but how well she was. The horror of losing her started to become more real as I saw her through other people's eyes. I'd kept myself emotionally from going there, but now she was at home, her threatened absence seemed more real and more distressing.

> With God we shall gain the victory,
> and he will trample down our enemies.
> (Psalm 60:12)

Martha took some convincing to stay in the same room as Hope, and it was only when she realised she was such a tiny baby and couldn't cry very loudly that she started to warm to her. After a frank conversation with my mother on a walk to a playgroup one day, Martha returned home seemingly content to have another sibling, and called her 'my baby sister, Hope' from then on. Jamie needed no encouragement showing his love to her, almost too physically at times, with kisses and strokes and squeezes.

When all three were together, I would feel awe rising up in my heart: 'I have three children,' I would remind myself. 'I have three children. How blessed am I? I have three children!' I would never take that fact for granted. 'My arms are full and my heart is full,' I noted in my diary.

At the same time, I was grateful I wouldn't have to face pregnancy again and was struggling constantly with painful blocked milk ducts due to the expressing. Pumping milk can make you feel like a cow! It all took time because of the careful washing and sterilising of equipment, and I wondered if I'd be able to continue once my parents left and I was alone looking after three little children while Paul was at work.

The end of his paternity leave came far too quickly. His work had graciously offered two weeks of compassionate leave in addition, had she died or been seriously unwell, but with such a well baby, he was back after two weeks; most of his paternity leave had been while we were in hospital.

> For you have been my refuge,
> a strong tower against the foe.
> (Psalm 61:3)

As well as awe and gratitude, I found myself feeling guilt – survivor's guilt. Why was Hope spared while all my friends in the SOFT community had had stillbirths? These kinds of questions have no answers, and I lived with the tension of acknowledging the heartbreak of what they'd been through existing simultaneously with our joy and delight. We weren't any more loved or blessed than them; often I don't think there even is an answer to 'Why?' Why did they get death when we got life? I don't know. This world is broken and it is beautiful. It is full of pain and full of love. Evil and goodness coexist and ultimately goodness will win out, but faith doesn't show in the sunny times. It only surfaces in the dark, lonely times when you truly find out what you believe. How we live our lives reflects what we believe about God, and what happens to us along the way isn't indicative of what He thinks or feels towards us. How we respond, however, shows a lot about our understanding of His goodness and intentions towards us.

Yes, my soul, find rest in God;
my hope comes from him.
(Psalm 62:5)

Both Paul and I found our bodies were responding to what we'd been through: he hurt his back putting on socks and I injured a leg trying to kick a heavy box along the floor. Had we stored up trauma in our bodies and it was beginning to seep out now? I joked he was waddling like me due to sympathy pains!

My brother, Ian, came to stay for a while, and we needed every extra pair of hands. Hope either napped in the sling or while being cuddled, and she still slept for a long time in the day, being so small! She made it up to 1.9 kilogrammes, or 4 pounds and 3 ounces, by the time she was eighteen days old, and we celebrated her new heaviness. Incredible, really, when she was actually still so tiny!

There seemed so much to get done now I was home. We needed to buy a chest of drawers for Jamie's clothes so Hope could have the drawers in the changing table – the kind of task we'd neglected in case she never came home, and we didn't want the empty drawers to be a tragic reminder of our loss. I had to register her at our GP surgery, and finding an appointment to register her birth was challenging due to the post-Covid backlog. The hospice had given us medication to be used in the scenario that Hope had been born at home and my father took it all to the local pharmacy to be destroyed. We were grateful she'd never needed any of it.

Two doctors visited us from the hospice and discharged Hope from the Specialist Palliative Care team. They told us how pleased everyone had been when they'd heard the news, as it can be rare to hear good news at a hospice. It was a bittersweet moment.

Because you are my help,
I sing in the shadow of your wings.
I cling to you;
your right hand upholds me.
(Psalm 63:7-8)

As Hope's due date of 16th March approached, I found I couldn't help but wonder what would have happened without the Trisomy diagnosis. Would I still be pregnant, struggling with hip pain and heartburn and exhaustion as the calendar tipped forty weeks? I couldn't imagine the physical strain of carrying a much bigger baby for longer, and felt it a kindness that I'd been spared a month or so of pregnancy.

I'd planned to post on social media to mark Hope's due date, writing something deep and insightful about our gratitude she was with us alive and healthy, but the day conspired against me. In the early hours of the morning she pulled the NG tube out, tearing the tape off her cheek and waking herself up to pain. I knew we couldn't get through to the community nurse team until working hours, so we offered her next feed in small instalments through a miniature bottle with a tiny teat. She seemed to feed well, which was very reassuring, and a nurse came at 9.30am to insert a new tube. Unfortunately, due to inexperience, nerves or the fact that Hope's nose was so small, she managed to scrape the back of Hope's throat, causing her great distress. It was upsetting to see the young nurse having to try again and again, made all the more difficult by Hope crying – crying that rarely ceased for the rest of that day. You can't explain or apologise to a small baby; you can only hold them close and cuddle them and speak in a reassuring tone of it all being over now. Perhaps I was speaking those words to a deep part of myself too.

> All people will fear;
> they will proclaim the works of God
> and ponder what he has done.
> (Psalm 64:9)

No one from the regional speech and language team had got in touch with us after we'd been home a full week, so I phoned until I chased someone down. It turned out the lady who'd been assigned to us had delayed contacting us, dreading having to see another T18 baby. She'd supported one before who had struggled terribly to feed and put on weight, and she had found the experience very difficult.

'Hope doesn't have Trisomy 18!' I was exasperated. 'That should never have been on the referral!' We'd been soldiering on with the tube-feeding because whoever filled in the form hadn't withheld diagnosis until the results came back. I was not impressed.

She apologised and came the next day. After enthusiastically observing Hope drink a full feed of forty millilitres of expressed breast milk, she gave us the go-ahead to continue bottle feeding. We never looked back. After three days of only bottle feeds and without consulting anyone else, we removed the tube ourselves and unceremoniously dumped it in the bin. It was marvellous to see her gorgeous face fully and it enabled everyone to see that she wasn't a sick baby, just a small one.

We started to take Hope out in the pram and began to witness what a special baby she was to so many people, as the caring ladies who worked at the kids' preschool crowded out to see her, and friends from church came into the car park to lean over the pram and see her dainty face. I was unwilling to take her indoors while so small, in case she picked up a virus, but still wanted to show her off!

A friend sent me this message:

> I'm continuing to pray for you and your beautiful little miracle. Hope's story is already such an incredible one and your faith throughout the process has truly inspired and convicted me. The night Hope was born was a big turning point for me as I had been very passive with my faith. And my husband, who is not a believer, said how this is the first time he has ever actually seen a miracle happen, and I've seen some changes in his approach to God. So thank you baby Hope and thank you Beth.

In response, I wrote in my diary:

This message has stunned me, in a good way. We never had the drive to make her life count for something or have a larger meaning. We were happy to love her as long as we had her and then release her to Jesus, trusting God knew the best place for her. I am so grateful He chose to give her back to us, so she can play with her siblings and know the love of all the extended family too. I hope she never feels a pressure to make her life count but is purely happy being loved by God and loving Him, knowing all her sins are forgiven and she is truly precious.

41
Adjusting

24th March 2022

> For you, God, tested us;
> you refined us like silver …
> we went through fire and water,
> but you brought us to a place of abundance …
> Praise be to God,
> who has not rejected my prayer
> or withheld his love from me!
> (Psalm 66:10, 12b, 20)

One practical way I'd changed since receiving that first fateful phone call with the test results was that I'd become a person who always answered my phone. Gone were the days when I never had the sound on because no one phoned me. This whole experience had made answering phone calls very important.

A call came through from a withheld number. It was the geneticist.

Our interaction went along these lines:

'Hello. How are you and Hope? All well? Great, that's good to hear. I was phoning to check that you'd got your results through?'

'No, we've not heard anything else,' I replied.

'Well, I have the results from the full genetic testing and I can tell you it's all come back as normal.'

'Normal': Hope had no detectable level of Trisomy 18 in her blood. I sat down on the bottom stair in the hallway to absorb this and to shield myself from the children's noise in the lounge. I breathed a deep sigh of relief – it was incredibly good news.

'Now remember,' the geneticist continued, 'the first test could detect if more than 20 per cent of the cells in her blood had the genetic condition and this one picks up between 10 and 20 per cent. Therefore, there is a possibility that under 10 per cent of the cells in her blood are affected, or that some other part of her body is. But what is your feeling, as you look at her, as her mother?'

'She seems like a completely ordinary newborn to me. I've not seen any reason for concern or anything unusual,' I replied.

'I think it is unlikely Hope has any form of mosaicism and it seems clear that there was something wrong with the placenta. Unfortunately, I do have some bad news. The biopsy of the placenta was taken to test for infection and was stored in a type of material that means it cannot now receive genetic testing.'

It took a few moments for me to grasp this. I tried to stifle an emerging panic and swallow the rising dread.

'No, that can't be the case. The placenta is the only way to find out if she doesn't have even a small level of mosaicism, right? I've been hoping and praying it would come back to confirm confined placental mosaicism and then we would know for sure and can get on with our lives.' I pleaded with the geneticist to change the narrative our story was starting to take: the continuing uncertainty of how T18 might affect our lives.

We believed that if Hope had even a small level of mosaicism, there was a high likelihood she could pass it on. She might never be able to have children, or at least have babies that lived very long, but we couldn't know. Would this affect future relationships for her? What if she fell for someone who wanted children so desperately that he didn't want to take the risk of remaining with her? Actually, I questioned, should we even tell her? We'd just spent a few months expecting an erroneous outcome and could have been saved the heartache of it all if we'd not known. Would it be better for her to not know she had a tiny chance of having some cells that have an extra chromosome, which might affect her fertility? How much worry and heartache could she be spared if we didn't tell her, as she probably wouldn't face these issues anyway? But what if she did? What if she faced repeated baby loss, only to find out we'd hidden all of this from her, never telling her about the complications in the pregnancy and their potential impact on her?

It was an ethical quandary I couldn't face on the limited amount of sleep I was getting, so I decided it would have to be shelved for now as it was in no way urgent. The trust I'd been exercising over the previous few months would have to be stretched out to last longer. Maybe this story wouldn't have a nice, neat ending; maybe I'd have to live with the possibility of our beloved daughter experiencing exactly what we had over and over again and I'd have to wait and see. It would be two to three decades before we might find out if her fertility was affected, and I wondered how I'd live with that potential impending heartbreak.

'God, help me to trust You. Help me not to worry about this but to leave it all in Your hands,' I whispered that night in bed. 'Although I really would like to have more information than we currently have. Can the non-genetic testing give that to us, Lord?'

After seeing such a miracle in Hope being born alive, I now had more faith and audacity to pray bigger prayers. The next day I prayed that we'd know for sure, one way or another, so we wouldn't have to live with the uncertainty, while I continued to submit it all to God. When Jesus faced his execution on a cross, He poured out His honest request to God, while also submitting His will,[40] so I felt I could ask God straight up to have a clear answer whether Hope had any level of mosaicism or not, while also saying I would continue to trust Him for her future even if we never knew.

---

[40] 'Father, if you are willing, take this cup from me; yet not my will, but yours be done' (Luke 22:42).

27th March 2022

Mother's Day: how different this day could have been this year!
Instead of struggling with loss, I'd started the day cuddled up in
bed with Hope asleep in the crook of my arm. We'd had a night
where she'd fed, had a nappy change and then lay contentedly
in the cot until sleep stole over her. Hearing her stir at dawn, I
picked her up and she settled again quickly, nestled next to me.
She continued to be a chilled, easy baby and had met more of
our extended family, as we'd hosted Paul's side for lunch the
day before.

I was reading a book that included a very well-known
passage in Christian circles, 1 Corinthians 13, or the 'love
chapter', and one verse jumped out at me, suddenly imbued
with new meaning: '[Love] always protects, always trusts, always
hopes, always perseveres' (1 Corinthians 13:7).

I saw the myriad ways we had loved Hope even before she
was born. We had *protected* her by choosing not to have a
termination, not risking an amniocentesis (although maybe one
would have been a good idea!) and not subjecting her to labour
and a natural birth, during which the placenta might have failed
and she could have died. We had *trusted* that God would be with
us and would show us His goodness no matter what happened,
and we trusted His word to us, *'There is no death in your body.'* We
had always *hoped* that she'd live, no matter what level of disability
she'd been born with. We had also *persevered*: we'd persevered
with the pregnancy, persevered in prayer, persevered in fighting
for her to receive the level of care a non-T18 baby would and
persevered in raising up prayer for her from our community.
She was deeply loved!

28th March 2022

> For you have been my hope, Sovereign LORD,
> my confidence since my youth.
> From my birth I have relied on you;
> you brought me forth from my mother's womb.

I will ever praise you.
I have become a sign to many;
you are my strong refuge.
(Psalm 71:5-7)

A breastfeeding specialist from the health visiting team called and talked me through how to transition from bottle to breast safely with such a tiny baby. She encouraged me to start a feed with the bottle to take the edge off Hope's hunger so she wasn't desperate for milk, offer a feed directly for a few minutes and then put her back on to the bottle for the remainder of the feed. We needed to know she was getting the full amount of milk each time and not tire her out too much with all the effort it took to suck and swallow.

'Babies are hard-wired to breastfeed,' she reassured me. 'Hope knows what to do!'

It was all the encouragement I needed.

Hope did well with this new pattern of feeding, but my enthusiasm was soon quenched by a phone call a week or so later from the dietician. Apparently, Hope's new weight of 4 pounds and 7 ounces was not on track. In their opinion, she wasn't putting on weight fast enough.

'Oral feeding uses a lot more energy, so Hope is burning more calories than when she was being tube-fed,' the dietician explained. Then they said something that stopped me in my tracks: 'The newborn phase will last a lot longer because she's so small.'

We didn't think we'd get a newborn phase at all and now we were getting extra! What a gift – it felt like such a blessing.

Hope took to breastfeeding well, which made my life a lot easier. We all got Covid over the Easter holidays and thankfully she wasn't too unwell with it. We'd escaped the virus up to that point, but now it was being allowed to circulate freely, it was impossible to dodge! We were all testing negative again by Easter Sunday, 17th April, and were asked to share our story at church. Now we'd got over Covid, I felt ready to expose her to a crowded room. As we shared the news from all the genetic results, there were not many dry eyes in the room. Paul shared some of the story from his perspective, and I realised I'd been so caught up in my own experience that I'd never stopped to consider his. He teared up as he talked about the harrowing drive to the hospital alone before she was born, having no idea what would face him when he arrived, or what would transpire that evening. It had been a brutal experience, there was no doubt about that.

The next day I wrote in my diary:

> When the earth and all its people quake,
> it is I who hold its pillars firm.
> (Psalm 75:3)

> I can't imagine what this last year would have looked like had we not had unshakeable faith in the Lord and in His goodness. Would we have even tried for a third without the image of Jesus in Gethsemane, knowing the suffering to come but counting it worthwhile? Would we have done the amniocentesis and found out it was confined placental mosaicism early on? Would we have hidden all this from others, rather than shared the journey? Would we have responded differently and would that have caused an irreparable rift in our marriage? All I know is that God held the pillars of our world firm and *He is good*.

20th April 2022

Something awful happened that left me deeply shaken. I found I was scared by how extreme my reaction was.

At home alone with the three kids, I had Hope in the Moses basket in the lounge while the other two were playing together when I remembered I'd left something in another room. Being unwilling to take all of them with me, I decided I could briefly nip out and be back before they noticed, assuming nothing would happen. Of course, I was wrong.

The moment I left the room, Jamie, in a burst of affection for Hope, decided to climb into the Moses basket to give her a cuddle. Not being the sturdiest piece of furniture, it hadn't been built to take the weight of a toddler hanging off one side and the base tipped over as he attempted to climb up. The basket, not attached to the base by design, flipped out and Hope ended up on the floor.

I heard a crash and a cry and raced into the room to find Hope facedown, inches away from the sharp edge of the granite fireplace surround. I immediately burst into tears, all the shock and horror of the past few months bursting out as I sobbed so hard I struggled to breathe. I felt a fierce rage towards Jamie for endangering Hope and I wanted to hurt him, which frightened me. I was intensely fearful as I picked her up from the floor, and wondered if she'd broken a limb or damaged her skull. I yelled at Jamie, making him cry harder as he flinched away from my anger, and Martha, a sensitive soul, started to cry because everyone else was crying.

I was shaking with fear and adrenaline, scared at the intensity of my own response. I tried to calm myself down, held Hope close to my chest and spoke reassuringly to Martha and Jamie until they quietened. Then I phoned Paul and asked what I should be looking out for with Hope.

'Is she crying? Is she moving her limbs like normal? Do you see any bumps on her head?'

Eventually it was clear that Hope hadn't been hurt by her tumble out of the cot, and I never left her alone in there again. I apologised to Jamie for the ferocity of my response and cuddled him as he cried, expressing the fear he'd felt from my outburst. I came away recognising afresh that I was not OK deep down. I came to understand I needed to draw it all out into the light, acknowledge the feelings I'd buried and determined to deal with after the event, and so start to heal. I couldn't respond with that level of anger the next time one of the children accidentally hurt Hope, and I couldn't ignore the depth of terror that experience had unmasked. It had unnerved me but also shown me I needed to pursue emotional healing and wholeness.

The hospice had kindly offered counselling for as long as I felt I needed. I didn't feel I deserved it, though, and I felt guilty for taking the counsellor's time from someone who was bereaved or was dealing with the daily difficulties of caring for a disabled child.

When we met for an initial consultation, my counsellor was able to allay those concerns, and as we talked over many months, she helped me to accept and own the fact we had been through profound trauma, and I allowed myself to call it that. Yes, Hope had lived and continued to thrive and develop normally, but those few months had been horrendous, and I could acknowledge that.

With the counsellor, I could dredge up the darkest and most painful feelings those few months had evoked and which I'd buried – first to survive and then because I felt the happy ending negated the previous trauma. I had to work through my anger at the consultants' bias and strong persuasion that there was no hope. I had to break down the protective layer of numbness I'd employed as a way to get through the day and keep turning up for my kids. Busyness had been an effective distraction as I'd not had time to contemplate the projected immediate future or dwell on the melee of emotions threatening to swell up at any point, but it was all there still, not too far under the surface and could be triggered easily.

I came to realise I never referred to the baby I'd carried in my womb as Hope, because Hope had come to exist in my mind at the moment of her birth. Pre-birth, I'd loved and bonded with a sickly little baby I was going to care and fight for, and who might never breathe or feed unaided. The counsellor helped me understand this baby was a figment of my imagination and had never existed: it had always been Hope I'd been pregnant with. I actually had to grieve the loss of this fictitious baby, one I had genuinely loved, and reconcile the baby I had been carrying in my womb with the baby I was now carrying in my arms. I still struggle to refer to the baby in utero as Hope because our expectations so mismatched reality.

I don't think I could have revisited the awful moments and written about them with honesty and clarity if I hadn't already done that in the safety the counsellor created for me. We knew the hospice care would make a huge difference, but we hadn't predicted that it would be through the counselling offered – how it would enable me to relive it all, make those memories safe and so release me to write.

42
Spring

22nd April 2022

> … we will tell the next generation
> the praiseworthy deeds of the LORD,
> his power, and the wonders he has done.
> (Psalm 78:4b)

Hope started smiling when she was almost two months old, wide-open unhindered smiles that melted my heart. She didn't weigh the same as an average newborn until she was three months old and was mistaken for a doll a number of times, giving passers-by a shock when the 'doll' I was carrying suddenly moved.

My first morning alone with all three started off rather dramatically with another water leak: water was gushing from our stop tap and flowing down the road. I called the wrong water board in my haste and had just got off the phone with the correct one when I heard a knock at the door. It was an engineer to tell me he'd fixed it. I looked at him, down at my phone and back at him.

'But I've only just phoned to report it…' I mumbled, startled at his speedy appearance.

'Oh, have you called it in?' he asked. 'I live around the corner and saw it on my way to work so thought I'd stop to have a look. It was a simple fix.'

Our road isn't a through road to anywhere and so it felt like an angel had happened to be flying past and saved me hours of stress and trouble by stopping to 'have a look'. I was very grateful the morning hadn't been dominated by the hassle of sorting out the leak.

1st May 2022

Hope was exclusively breastfeeding by May, although a slowing down in weight gain after having Covid prompted the dieticians to recommend a high-calorie formula top-up.

I had her naps and feeds on a schedule, with most of her naps happening in the sling, as I had to take the older kids to preschool and it was easier to have her strapped to my front for the transition in and out of the house. I also thought fresh air and exercise would be good for us as we walked down and back again. A deeper reason was wanting to keep her close to me, as physically close as possible, whenever she was asleep, so I knew she was well. I could feel her breathing and warmth, and the reassurance gave me peace.

Standing in church on my mother's birthday, I found myself overcome with gratitude and wonder as I suddenly realised that the God of the Bible is a God who raises children from the dead to give them back to their parents. I thought of Elijah, who raised the widow's son (1 Kings 17:7-24), Elisha raising the Shunammite woman's son (2 Kings 4:8-37), Jesus raising a widow's son at the son's funeral (Luke 7:11-17) and Jarius' daughter (Mark 5:21-43). In each account, it was the grief of the parent that stirred compassion in the heart of the prophet or of Jesus Himself and prompted them to pray. God deeply cares about the grief of parents who have lost children. It breaks His heart too. Why some children survive terminal illnesses and live and some don't, I can't answer, but I do know that before sin came into the world and once His kingdom is fully established, there was and will be no death.

> 'He will wipe every tear from their eyes. There will be no more death' or mourning or crying or pain, for the old order of things has passed away.
> (Revelation 21:4)

5th May 2022

I will praise you, Lord my God, with all my heart;
I will glorify your name for ever.
For great is your love towards me;
you have delivered me from the depths,
from the realm of the dead …
for you, LORD, have helped me and comforted me.
(Psalm 86:12-13; 17b)

As I was pouring water onto Hope in the bath, I was suddenly very aware of the fact she was alive. She was alive and vibrant and gorgeous and smiley. There was no denying the fact she was here and very much made her presence known. Like at the doctor's surgery when she needed her first set of immunisations and screamed very loudly. The poor doctor had to calculate how much Calpol she could have because she was still so small: 2.84 kilogrammes, or 6 pounds and 4 ounces.

A moment that became a milestone to celebrate was when we were able to register her birth after the COVID-19 enforced delay and leave with a birth certificate. This single piece of paper, so light to hold, held a huge weight in its symbolism and meaning for us.

11th May 2022

There were other moments that were equally as memorable but slightly less distinguished. One such incident was when I was breastfeeding Hope on the sofa when Jamie told me he needed to use the toilet. He dutifully followed my instructions to fetch the potty, planted it right by my feet and left a rather large gift in it. Which stank. Martha then decided she needed to empty her bowels, ran to the bathroom and after a few minutes started yelling in her sing-song voice, 'I'm finished!'

So there I was, trapped feeding Hope, unable to escape the stench of Jamie's deposit, also needing to attend to Martha, when Hope decided to join in and released more than her nappy could contain. It helpfully oozed out of her clothes and onto my sleeve. Jamie, meanwhile, started pottering around with his trousers and pants around his ankles while I desperately asked him not to sit down before I'd had a chance to wipe his bottom.

I honestly did not know where to begin. I thought to myself, 'All I need now is the doorbell to ring with a delivery requiring a signature and I'll be done!'

Lovely memories included the children really taking to Hope. Jamie tried to reassure her once when she was crying by saying, 'It's OK, Baby, we'll take care of you.' He read a book to her by pointing to the pictures and telling her what the objects were. Martha would collect and deliver cuddly toys to her in the bouncer chair; one time, I turned around from washing up to find Hope almost buried beneath the pile of offerings!

> Unless the LORD had given me help,
> I would soon have dwelt in the silence of death.
> When I said, 'My foot is slipping,'
> your unfailing love, LORD, supported me.
> When anxiety was great within me,
> your consolation brought me joy.
> (Psalm 94:17-19)

43
Living with Hope

Summer 2022

I have a theory that the sleep deprivation you suffer as a parent of a newborn hinders you from forming long-term memories, so you forget how challenging it is.

Reading back through my diary of Hope's first few months was a good reminder of how difficult it can be to have your sleep disturbed constantly, especially when your days are filled with looking after older children, so you're unable to catch up on rest. You look forward to the nights to get some quiet, only to be up nursing and comforting a hungry and windy baby, and so the cycle repeats.

I found I experienced a range of emotions. I was, of course, deeply grateful Hope was thriving. We were living a reality far beyond our wildest dreams when we brought her home with no medication and no real ongoing concerns. On the other hand, we did have three preschoolers, which meant we were outnumbered by rather dependent beings who loved to express their demands and grievances as loudly as possible, and each wanted one-on-one attention a lot of the time!

I found myself thinking, 'This goes so fast because you haven't got a chance to sit down and catch your breath or have any time for yourself!'

Another friend who has three children with similar age gaps once told me she coped by writing off two years per child. The first two years of their life might be manic and full on, but hang on in there and you'll get through it. I was grateful for that advice during the nights we decided it'd be best to assume we wouldn't get any sleep when the kids tag-teamed wake-ups.

Hope laughed for the first time just before she was four months old, and it was the most magical sound. We were all in the car and I was sat in the back next to her, smiling at her smiling at me, when she gurgled a little giggle in response to me chuckling at her. Everyone got very excited and praised her highly, then the fight was on for who could get her to laugh again.

A few days later, I heard through the SOFT community that the lady with the twins had given birth: the little boy with full T18 had lived for an hour and his sister was doing well. It was sobering to continuously receive the news of babies' deaths, but I felt it was right and fitting to stay part of the SOFT community and bear witness to these losses. Each one was a valued, loved child who was wanted, and each bereaved parent showed incredible bravery in carrying the pregnancy until the end. I wanted to stand with and acknowledge their pain and heartbreak as well as the life and death of their child.

About a month into weekly Zoom calls with the counsellor from the hospice, I was sharing about the birth and I suddenly had a realisation. I recorded it in my diary like this:

> Talked with my counsellor about how friends had been gathered over Zoom to pray at the exact moment of Hope's birth. Only realised today they were prepared to be informed of a newborn baby's death, right at that moment. What incredible friends to stand with us and not turn away in our (potentially) darkest hour. Instead of grieving with us, what a celebration they were invited to! They were 'there' live at the moment of victory. Lord God, bless those friends!

We still hadn't heard anything from the non-genetic testing on the placenta, and I was holding out hope and trusting it would have some key piece of information we didn't have yet. As it was our only way of confirming the diagnosis of CPM and thereby freeing Hope of the spectre of T18 haunting her future pregnancies, I placed a lot of importance on it. It constantly felt like a missing piece of the puzzle, a piece I needed to have full closure.

We had an appointment with Hope's paediatrician, Dr Grant, booked for halfway through August and I assumed he'd have the results. I had no idea how else to access them or who I should pursue to get hold of them. So I waited and prayed and waited some more.

Eventually our meeting with Dr Grant came and I strode in confidently with Hope, knowing he'd be impressed with her development and that now she'd started eating so well, she was on the graph for weight and not charting her own course off it.

He didn't have the results. He assumed they'd gone to the obstetrics team and he said he'd follow up to find out. He also didn't have a clear route for moving forward as there was no precedent set for a child like Hope. He suggested we book a heart scan to make sure the ASD had closed as expected, invite the geneticist to see Hope again, and offered to make a referral to the child development team (CDT).

'She doesn't actually fit any of the criteria, but seeing as this is such an unusual case, they might accept it.'

Life continued as normal while we waited for all of these appointments.

13th September 2022

Diary entry:

> Hope's passport arrived in the post on my birthday. A perfectly timed present, reminding us what a gift she is. What a gift all of our children are. Emotional moment looking at her passport picture – the baby who wasn't supposed to survive – the baby who was going to have such complex medical needs she'd never be able to travel internationally. And here we are. Six and a half months old, developing well, piling on the pounds. Her life will always be a testament to God's love and power: His kindness,

goodness, faithfulness and ability to heal. What a wonderful God we serve!

18th September 2022

Church services could be hugely emotional: as the band played 'Way Maker',[41] a song I'd listened to on repeat during the pregnancy, the feeling of now cuddling a healthy Hope meant I was so choked up I could barely sing. Previously, I'd sung it in faith, and now the words took on new meaning and power as we sang them having come through the storm. Her physical presence and health could not be denied, and we could only give glory to God.

The talk was about the 'suddenly' moments of God, when He breaks in and changes a situation. The speaker, Dr David Bennett,[42] talked of how facing the grief and hard times head on, rather than trying to escape them, can allow God to come in and transform them. It felt like he was talking about Hope. Then our pastor invited people to come up to share, and I couldn't resist. I had to talk about what God had done! And it wasn't only in terms of how we had stood at the edge of the lions' den or the fiery furnace and saw God deliver life out of death,[43] but also the way the church had supported us through it all. Our community hadn't backed down or left us isolated in our grief; they'd stood with us – and look at how God had answered, He 'who is able to do immeasurably more than all we ask or imagine' (Ephesians 3:20)!

It made me reflect on how the devil had worked so hard to kill Moses and Jesus as babies,[44] heartbreakingly eliminating an entire generation of boys each time, and their lives had had an

---

[41] Sinach, 'Way Maker', Mayolee; see this version by Leeland, Integrity Music, www.youtube.com/watch?v=29IxnsqOkmQ (accessed 17th December 2024).

[42] Author of *A War of Loves*, Grand Rapids, MI: Zondervan, 2018; www.dacbennett.com (accessed 5th December 2024).

[43] Daniel 6; Daniel 3.

[44] Exodus 1:22; Matthew 2:13-16.

incredible eternal impact. While I do not want to compare Hope to these men of the Bible, it reminded me of how her life is a sign and wonder that points to God's goodness and healing power.

I'd also been reading a book with some friends which issued a challenge that I knew I needed to accept: 'When we pray for healing and God heals, we shouldn't act like it didn't happen.'[45] I included this quote when we dedicated Hope at church at the end of September: we had prayed for life and God had granted it.

2nd October 2022

Diary entry:

> I found myself lying awake last night, feeling haunted – tormented even – by the thought another family might have terminated the pregnancy with Hope on the information we were given. I don't know what would have happened if we'd gone down that route; I don't know if we would have had to have an amniocentesis. I took it to the Lord in prayer as I couldn't shake the feeling that was so disturbing me. I felt God reassure me, 'That is why I chose you to be her parents.' He chose us to be her parents so that she'd live, knowing we'd choose and fight for life for her. He entrusted her to us so that she'd live. It brought me great peace.

The next day we took Hope to Paul's workplace to show her off, and I found myself unable to stop ruminating on some of his colleagues' comments when we'd announced we were continuing the pregnancy: Some had been astonished we weren't going to terminate, although all had been very supportive. Introducing Hope at his place of work felt a show of defiance to the part of the medical world who'd written her

---

[45] Stormie Omartian, *The Power of a Praying Parent*, Eastbourne: Kingsway, 1996, p95.

off and decided a baby with a possible genetic condition wasn't worthy of life.

'Here she is!' I wanted to proclaim. 'Alive and well! And even if she wasn't, she'd still be loved, and worthy of having a chance at life!'

It felt like a victory, displayed a living and healthy baby in place of the absence we'd been expecting, yet perhaps a hollow victory, as I wasn't sure any opinions were changed. Confirmation bias would project on to her that she was so unique and unusual a story that no others would be affected; the medical world would tick along as before and write off Trisomy babies without a second thought. In my core, I knew I had to meet with the foetal medicine consultants, but I didn't have the courage. I feared being patronised and didn't want to face the conflict I was expecting it to be, so I let decision inertia win out. Yes, I felt like a coward, but I was also too busy to think about it very much, and let myself be carried on the flow of the full days of motherhood.

44
Future hope

6th October 2022

Paul questioned whether it was necessary to see the geneticist again because surely there would be no new information they could give us. While I understood his reasoning, in my heart I felt there were still loose ends and it was worth seeing if they had any more answers. If we had no more appointments now, this would be the end of the story and we would still have no results from the testing on the placenta and not know if and how much Hope might be affected by mosaicism.

In preparing for the appointment, I rifled through the pile of letters and papers that I'd kept pertaining to Hope and the pregnancy. I'd always meant to sort through it, but as a mother of three young ones, those kinds of non-urgent tasks were always delayed. I was looking for the original appointment letter to double check where to go in the hospital and came across the black and white photos from the twelve-week scan in the pile.

I was immediately overcome with emotion and burst into tears.

I had been so blasé about the early scan that I hadn't kept the photos anywhere in particular and had thought I'd lost them. After we'd got the diagnosis, I was close to panicking as I searched for those photos, thinking they might be the only physical ones we'd have of her alive. They felt so priceless and treasured when I did find them, and I made sure I kept them safe. Being presented with these photos again reminded me of that sense of relief, but now instead of just a few scan photos, we had her: a whole, living, breathing baby! As well as the thumbs-up photo, there was one of her holding the back of her hand to her forehead in a very dramatic pose. *Yes, little one, you most certainly caused a lot of drama!*

I had so many questions for the geneticist, and overriding them all was a desire for certainty. I wanted to know 100 per cent if Hope had any level of Edwards' or not. Decades of not knowing and then potential heartache when trying for a baby seemed a heavy burden to bear.

I prayed very honestly that night, 'Lord, look, I just want certainty. I know I can't have it, but I have to tell you: I just want certainty.'

I assumed that certainty could only come in the form of results from the infection testing on the placenta. I knew it was highly unlikely but desperately hoped there were some answers for us. I was forgetting that sometimes our prayers are answered in ways we could never expect.

7th October 2022

I felt nervous driving to the appointment. My head was telling me this was potentially a waste of time and NHS resources, but my heart was clinging to the image of the geneticist as a kind of gatekeeper. The information they'd given us before had helped us to understand what was likely to have happened during the pregnancy, and I was wishing for the same thing again. I knew it was unlikely, but it felt like it was now or never. No one else had been able to give us answers or explanations, and at least the opportunity for receiving new information was present if we met in person.

This is how I remember the consultation going.

We spent the forty minutes of the appointment in conversation with each other and interactions with Hope. The geneticist agreed it looked highly likely it was confined placental mosaicism because Hope clearly was developing completely normally, and she explained how the NIPT test is relatively new in the UK so there is a level of inexperience in interpreting it. They told me how, because of the prevalence of testing in their home country they'd seen cases like Hope's before. Apparently it was more likely for a baby to be born with CPM, rather than mosaicism, as there was a higher likelihood of the latter pregnancies not making it to full term.

In the geneticist's opinion, we should have been offered an amniocentesis to help plan the best course of care for the baby, rather than it being presented as confirming the diagnosis to aid the decision of whether to terminate or not. It would have told us it was mosaicism and so we could have had the placenta stored correctly for genetic testing at birth. Their concern was with the potential withholding of care at birth, had Hope needed any interventions. For example, because the medical team were expecting a baby who might die, had Hope got into any difficulties, they might not have fought as hard to save her. Therefore, 'having a baby who might die' would have become a self-fulfilling prophecy, even if it actually hadn't been inevitable. It was a chilling thought. However, I am still not sure we would have had an amnio, if we could go back in time and make that choice again. I was so averse to risk.

The geneticist told me they had fed back to the foetal medicine team at the specialist hospital and that they'd been 'very surprised' to hear the news. The team had asked for permission to look again at the scan photos they'd taken and I said that was fine. I certainly hoped there would be learning taken from this.

'It's hard, though,' I mentioned towards the end, 'not knowing if she has any cells affected. It's hard to think of how it might affect her future.'

'What do you mean?' the geneticist pressed.

'Well, I'd hate to think of her going through what we did, or only having babies with Edwards' who might not live very long.'

'Oh no, it doesn't get passed on. It's not hereditary.'

With one sentence, the outlook of our future shifted once again.

I assumed I looked shocked because they carried on explaining, 'It's like Down syndrome. It occurs by chance at conception, and although people with Edwards' don't tend to have babies because,' the geneticist paused delicately, 'they don't tend to live long enough, we know from adults with Down syndrome that they can have babies without it.'

I was overjoyed and shed a few tears. It felt like real closure, a proper ending to our story.

Even with no results from the placenta, even if we'd never know for sure if Hope had a tiny amount of the condition, I had the certainty I was so desperately craving. She couldn't pass it on. She wouldn't have babies with T18. There would be no painful conversations about this with her or with a future partner threatening the future. We were done and dusted with T18.

There's a story in the book of Daniel in the Old Testament of three young men who are captured and threatened with death if they do not serve the gods of the country they have been exiled to or worship an image of gold. The king is so confident, he proclaims, 'What god will be able to rescue you from my hand?'

They refuse, replying, 'King Nebuchadnezzar, we do not need to defend ourselves before you in this matter. If we are thrown into the blazing furnace, the God we serve is able to deliver us from it, and he will deliver us from Your Majesty's hand. But even if he does not, we want you to know, Your Majesty, that we will not serve your gods or worship the image of gold you have set up' (Daniel 3:15b, 16-18).

We'd expressed a similar sentiment during the pregnancy: 'We know God can deliver this baby alive, but even if He doesn't, we won't deny or forsake Him.'

The story continues to tell of how the king was so angered by their response, he ordered the furnace to be heated seven times hotter than usual and for the three men to be tied up and thrown in, fully clothed. It was so hot that even the soldiers who had thrown them in were killed.

In an instant the king was up on his feet in amazement because he could see 'four men walking around in the fire, unbound and unharmed, and the fourth looks like a son of the gods'. He called them to come out of the fire and 'the fire had not harmed their bodies, nor was a hair of their heads singed; their robes were not scorched, and there was no smell of fire on them'. The king ended by praising their God, saying that 'no other god can save in this way' (Daniel 3:25, 27, 29b).

This story was prominent in my mind as I drove home. We'd emerged from a fiery trial and there was not even the smell of smoke on us: no lingering negative impact at all. How had we come through so unscathed? I was astonished, grateful and humbled.

9th October 2022

Diary entry:

> I cried during worship at church today. I don't remember the song or the lyrics. I was standing holding Hope in the far back corner, seeing others standing and not singing. I prayed for the Holy Spirit to move, to create a powerful and worshipful environment. Then I was suddenly struck with awe and wonder at what God has done for Hope, that she is fine, she is free, and we have certainty. He has been so gracious. I sang at the top of my voice, stamping and punching the air, until I couldn't sing for crying. God did this for us. They came out of the fire and even their clothes did not smell of smoke. No lasting effects at all. Just the knowledge of the Presence of the Person of Jesus in the midst of our greatest trial, our hardest battle. And seeing His goodness played out over and over again. Thank You, Lord. How could I ever thank God enough?

> I've been reading *Growing Pains* by Dr Mike Shooter and the chapter I read last night talked of the unknown in medicine and how doctors shouldn't try to create certainty:

>> One final thought. The lower left quadrant of the [Johari] Window is the Unknown, where neither adults nor children know what is happening now or what might happen in the future. I have spent a lot

of time persuading paediatricians that it is not a sign of weakness to admit their ignorance. They should not invent certainties to fill the gap.[46]

Paediatricians… and foetal medicine consultants!

---

[46] Dr Mike Shooter, *Growing Pains: Making Sense of Childhood*, London: Hodder & Stoughton, 2018, p68.

45
Feedback meeting

9th January 2024

Paul had taken the day off for us to attend a meeting at the local hospital with both foetal medicine consultants. It had been organised by the head of the child development team who had been so impacted by Hope's story that she'd been using a family story about the experience, which I had written, in teaching sessions for junior doctors. I'd finally got the courage to acknowledge I did need this meeting to go ahead for me to move on fully. I needed to know they knew Hope didn't have T18.

I was apprehensive. It felt like taking sour-tasting medicine: you know it's good for you and you have to do it, but you'd really rather not.

I kept telling myself I'd feel better afterwards. I'd be able to have complete closure and move on. Yet I still felt that low-level anxiety churning in my gut. I found myself worrying they'd cancel and we'd have to reschedule, or it'd be postponed indefinitely and cast a looming shadow over my future of a dreaded event that never came and so always caused worry and stress.

The night before the meeting, as I prayed about it and asked for the strength and courage to share all I needed to say, I felt a little prompt to pray for the ground to be softened. For something to have happened, especially in the life of Dr Brown, to prepare them to hear our feedback and take it on board.

Paul and I had spent the evening discussing what we wanted to say. I had two lists of feedback – one from a year previously when I'd been in the thick of counselling and I'd scribbled down all I wanted to tell the consultants, and it was raw and spiky. 'Would you tell me with so little empathy that one of my already born children had an inoperable brain tumour and was going to die?!'

The second set I'd written over Christmas when I'd had some time to sort through the pile of scan notes and letters. I'd kept every single item pertaining to Hope, scared that they might be all that remained of her: precious mementoes of scan photos and hospital letters that would probably be discarded sometime after a live, healthy birth. This feedback was more measured and from a healthier, more whole place – a place that recognised doctors have an extremely difficult job, facing emotionally devastating events, and have to harden themselves to some extent to survive. Both Paul and I had read a book over the Christmas holiday called *Also Human* by Caroline Elton, a psychologist who counselled junior doctors in their career paths and was given a fascinating and often sad look into the way they learned to cope, or not:

> We regularly require doctors to carry out extraordinarily distressing tasks with inadequate attention given to their psychological well-being. Then we blame doctors when their psychological defences kick in, and they respond to patients or relatives with a lack of empathy.[47]

It was helpful for Paul and me to hash out exactly what it was I was wanting to say and condense it down to a few points. We decided it would be helpful to open with listing all the things we were grateful for under the care of this hospital and to emphasise we weren't bringing a complaint. We decided to explain I felt I needed to have this conversation to be able to move on, not only to hopefully improve care for anyone else who might find themselves in our position, but also to know

---

[47] Caroline Elton, *Also Human: The Inner Lives of Doctors*, London: William Heinemann, 2018, p309.

what would have happened had we chosen to terminate. I needed confirmation that they would not have let me do it; they wouldn't have allowed us to go down that route without further testing.

I wrote my list of positives, which included being seen quickly by the consultants once abnormalities were spotted at a routine scan; not offering termination again once we'd said we wouldn't consider one; letting us know about SOFT UK and the hospice; allowing me to be seen at home by the home birth team even though I was no longer able to have a home birth; the referral to the specialist hospital; and Hope's life being saved by having regular CTGs at the end of the pregnancy and the frequent scans.

My list of negatives started with the lack of empathy, and I noted phrases such as, 'I'm sorry to have to tell you this…' or, 'This is going to be hard to hear…' as helpful ways to couch the news. My second main point was the information overload in the scan after the diagnosis, describing how the emotional impact of hearing my baby was going to die made me shut down, and the lists of complications and decisions to be made were totally overwhelming. I also wanted to share how it felt that termination had been made to seem like the kindest and most logical option, even though we never thought we'd ever consider it. What would have happened had we said we wanted to terminate on the information we were given?

The morning dawned and it felt strange being back at the hospital after such an interval. It will always be the place all three of my children were born and where I'd lived for almost two weeks with my youngest, experiencing such a range of emotions with all the news we'd received there.

The head of the child development team, Dr Hammond, was already in the Maternity Education Department where we were meeting, and two other female members of staff soon joined. One young lady introduced herself to us as the patient safety midwife who was standing in for the Governance Lead, and the foetal medicine consultants arrived a few minutes later. No one was wearing face masks and it was good to see their full faces, making them feel less like strangers.

I tried to smile and show we were there to be friendly and constructive rather than angry and accusatory. Paul was drawing figures on the whiteboard with Hope and had a pile of books and toys ready to occupy her throughout the meeting.

Again, I've created the dialogue from what I remember rather than having recorded exactly what was said. I had thought about asking if I could take a recording because I was already in the process of writing this book, but I assumed they would either say no or feel restricted in their speech and edit themselves. I knew I couldn't record the conversation secretly and so trusted I'd remember what was said that was important to me.

'Is anyone chairing?' Paul started the conversation and, with looks around to show a no, I offered to open the floor with my notes.

'We have read your family story,' Dr Brown said. 'Thank you for that. It was good to read and hear about your experience.' The consultant looked me directly in the eye, with an open and humble manner.

'Yes,' Dr Hammond said. 'I sent it to them beforehand.'

I was taken aback: the prayer had been answered as the ground had absolutely and completely been prepared.

'Oh wow, I didn't know you were going to read that. I guess you'll know a lot of what I'm going to say, then!' I joked. Did this meeting even need to happen if they'd read that? Would they think this a waste of time? 'First of all, thank you for your time today. We're not here to make a complaint, but feel it'd be helpful to provide some feedback for future parents and to talk through what would have happened had we wanted to terminate. Of course, if Hope hadn't lived, we wouldn't be here as we'd be grieving still, so we feel we're in a unique position to share some thoughts that hopefully will made things a bit easier for anyone who has a similar diagnosis.'

I launched straight into my list of positives and all that we felt had gone well, and then started on my list of things we would have appreciated being done differently. After I'd finished, I asked Paul if he had anything to share, and he did.

He talked about his granny and how she'd lost a baby at birth (we weren't sure if it was a stillbirth or if the baby had been born with life-limiting disabilities and then died soon after), but after going through labour and giving birth, this baby was whisked away from her. His granny had never had a chance to hold or see the baby, and was afforded no opportunity to bond with or say goodbye to them. It was seen as the right thing to do in those days, more than seventy years ago now, to spare the mother the pain of seeing their baby so still and lifeless, but they were never able to grieve properly. We'd been told she had developed problems sleeping after that and relied on sleeping tablets for the rest of her life. What had been seen as a kindness had actually caused a deep anguish from which she never fully recovered.

'I wonder if what we see as kindness these days is sparing the parents the pain of continuing a pregnancy by choosing to end it sooner and therefore short-circuit the suffering? As a GP, I see the impact of ongoing trauma, and it makes me wonder if allowing nature to take its course takes away the question of, "What would have happened if we hadn't terminated?" Continuing a pregnancy allows the parents to feel no sense of guilt or responsibility because they weren't involved in the decision of when the pregnancy would end or, speaking more bluntly, when the baby would die.'

Hope was flicking through a pile of books, seated on his lap as he spoke – an undeniable presence in the room of what continuing a pregnancy can result in. She babbled away, pointing at various pictures as if she was telling him what the items were called.

Dr Brown responded to us first. 'First of all, thank you for coming in to share with us, and I would like to start by saying that everyone we see is an individual and their situations are unique. Another family might have responded differently to what you experienced and have made different choices. As to getting it wrong, we all make mistakes. I do acknowledge that when you receive bad news, you can feel emotionally overwhelmed, and that it can be hard to take in any more information, so I would like to offer an apology to you for that.'

I had not been expecting any sort of apology at all. I'd been geared for confrontation and conflict, and again felt taken aback. 'Thank you,' I responded. 'That's kind of you.' The consultant's humility was fast reconfiguring my opinion of them as some kind of emotionless monster, and I was glad I'd already written about the silent scan with them in case I'd been tempted to tone it down now we'd met again. Had they become a more humble person since we'd first met, or was my memory of our interaction skewed?

'We are in a tricky position,' Dr Brown shared, 'because people come in for a happy scan, to see their baby and find out the gender, and then we have the unenviable role of having to tell them something is wrong.'

'And times have changed a lot,' Dr Richards chipped in. 'In the past, there was little support for families with children with genetic conditions and now there are charities who, as you found, offer a lot of peer support and expert help to those who choose to continue their pregnancies. Remember, I did try to make the scans a good experience for you, forgetting all this silly business with the diagnosis but giving you the chance to see the baby and bond and make memories.'

As she spoke, I realised I'd not listed that as a positive. I'd taken it for granted and forgotten about it, rather than appreciated her affirming tone and outlook. I guess she hadn't questioned the diagnosis after the scan with the specialist, but she hadn't been negative or focused on how bad things could be.

'Things have also come a long way since we first had screening tests,' she continued. 'We used to have a script to learn and everyone would say the same thing. Without you having had the amniocentesis, it was a bit of a disaster to get the news and obviously changed the course of the pregnancy! You did also choose not to have the earlier screening test.'

I reassured her we hadn't refused that test due to any strong convictions and, to be honest, we were glad we hadn't had it in the long run, as it might have ruined more of the pregnancy. T18 could have been our overarching narrative from much earlier and we were spared that.

'That early blood test is more than just screening for syndromes,' Dr Brown explained. 'It also more accurately dates the pregnancy and can show us other things too. The value now is choice, so parents can make an informed decision, whatever that decision is.'

'Can I share what I am taking away from this conversation?' piped up a lady seated at the end of the table. 'I'm on the screening team and I wanted to say that we do come across people from all outlooks and so sometimes we do get it wrong. What I've understood from this conversation is that the NIPT test is a screening not diagnostic test, which is good to understand. I also wanted to share with you that we get feedback from the Down syndrome community and they ask us not to use phrases like, "I'm sorry to tell you," because they don't want it to be seen in a negative light. Of course, the syndromes are different, but you can see the position we're put in.'

'Oh, I see, that is tricky,' I replied, understanding more about the nature of the difficulty they can find themselves in, remembering to change their language and communication for different conditions. 'It's not quite the same, but I do understand what you're trying to say... What would have happened if we'd decided, on the information we were given, that we wanted to terminate?' I went on. 'You know, Hope is my delight, and I find I'm haunted by the thought we could have ended her life and that it would have been our choice.'

Dr Brown quickly replied, 'We would have strongly encouraged a diagnostic test to know for sure, which would have shown us we were dealing with mosaicism.'

'And we would have referred you to the tertiary hospital for them to advise you,' added Dr Richards.

At the time of this meeting, it had been two and a half years since the NIPT test had been introduced on the NHS, and I assume a greater level of experience in interpreting it and sharing its results had been gained. Other things had changed too.

'There is now a counselling room in the antenatal screening corridor,' Dr Brown shared with me, 'because we don't have the time in such a pressured environment to deal with parents after a consultation, so there's a private space now they can go and cry and talk.'

'That's a such a good idea. It is hard to be faced with happy, healthy pregnancies in the waiting room,' I replied.

'Yes. As much as we'd like to be separate from the normal scans, there isn't room in the hospital for that and so, unfortunately, the waiting room is the same, and we can't help that.'

We discussed other things not on my agenda which came up as we talked. They told us speaking with the specialist nurse before the birth and having a tour of SCBU was a unique plan for us, as was meeting the bereavement midwife.

'We could make those into care pathways so we know what to offer should parents choose to continue a pregnancy in your situation again,' was a suggestion made.

Conversation continued about adding a flag to patients' notes to indicate the presence of such a diagnosis so the mother wouldn't have to keep explaining to everyone they met what they were facing, and as the conversation drew to a close, Dr Richards asked me, 'What do you want us to take away from this meeting?'

I had to stop and think.

'I think one of the main things was how the baby was treated. For example, when I called the hospice, one of the first things the nurse said to me was, "Congratulations on your pregnancy." It signalled to me her depth of understanding of the value of this baby.' Even after all this time, I could feel the emotion well up and tears sting the backs of my eyes as that kindness tore through the lack of empathy we felt we'd experienced.

'And,' I continued, 'if a couple or parent chooses not to have an amniocentesis, then we really don't know the outcome. And, even though confined placental mosaicism is rare, to still explain there is a range of outcomes for babies with conditions like Edwards' so we don't know for sure what's going to happen.'

The meeting ended positively and we were thanked warmly for taking the time to come and share our feedback. I felt exceedingly tired for the rest of the day, even though it had all gone so much better than we'd expected, and it took a few days to realise something that meeting had sparked in me.

The meeting had sparked a realisation that I did not regret what we'd been through. I did not wish we could turn back time and either refuse to take the NIPT test or have an amniocentesis. I had learned that no matter what you go through, no matter how dark the night, you are never alone if you put your trust in God, 'for darkness is as light to you' (Psalm 139:12). Our dark times are where we can find ourselves hidden in Him, tucked up like a baby bird in 'the shadow of your wings' (Psalm 17:8). He often doesn't answer our prayers in the timing or method we'd like, but hindsight always shows up that He's right.

I appreciated the life experience we'd gained and how it had changed me, as a person, into someone who could now stand with others in their suffering and grief, without attempting to diminish or downplay it. Someone who could support others through tough seasons of ill health or grief, having known a little of what they were going through, while being spared the depth of it myself. I appreciated getting to know the SOFT UK community and the brave parents who mourn or care for

Edwards' babies. I felt for those who found the courage to try again after loss, facing the fear day in, day out, of something happening to take this baby too.

A mother's love is real. It cannot be denied. What does she not give up for her children: her body, her sleep, her leisure activities, her identity, her career progression, her pelvic floor, her tummy muscles, her friendships, her evenings and her outside interests? What will she not fight to protect her babies?

May I always be a Mama Bear for you, my children, and may you always feel my arms of love and protection surrounding you, day in and day out, just as God's arms encircle mine.

Postscript
Writing

I wrote this book in snatches, in stolen pockets of time where I could be uninterrupted and undisturbed. I relied on family members to look after the kids while I slipped away and wrote. It couldn't be short periods of time. I needed long enough stretches to read my diary entry from that day, enter into the memories and emotions and then write; to get into the flow where time and outward distractions dropped away and the urgency to tell Hope's story took over.

I hadn't planned when I first started writing a diary at age fifteen that one day I would use it as a reference point and memory aid to write a book. It's amazing how much of a traumatic experience we forget or blank out. I remembered some of the events recorded here vividly, word for word, while other parts were gone. As I read through the diary entry for each day and began to relive the episodes, memories resurfaced and fleshed themselves out. They weren't erased, just unrecoverable until accessed. Then it was all there – the thoughts and feelings and questions. I'm sure my brain has filled in some of the recollections, like a partially completed colouring-in picture, supplementing reality where there were blank spaces. These events may be remembered differently by others, but this is as accurate a recall as I could create.

I knew I had a great story to tell, but my life was so full and so busy after Hope was born, there was no chance to write. I did want to document the whole story, even if it was only for Hope herself to know the incredible build-up to her birth, but I also knew I was unlikely to find the time. I was asked to write her story for one of the charities; they give me a deadline, which was the prompt I needed to write an overview, capturing most of the highlights and difficult points, but I knew it only skimmed the surface. I wanted to delve the depths and share the full story. At the same time, I recognised many of the episodes were terribly painful, and I recoiled from engaging with those memories and the emotions they'd expose.

The desires warred. It would have been easier to move on and let it become a story that got told occasionally at dinner parties – a story Hope would never truly understand the full import of until I'd passed away and she may read through my diaries and then share the trauma of what we went through.

I asked God to give me the fire in my bones, to compel me to find the time to write the story.

The next day I spoke to someone whose baby had been deemed 'incompatible with life' so she felt she had to terminate. A book I was reading featured the story of a young lady who had the same story: terminal diagnosis at a scan, termination and then she experienced a deep depression. Even a well-known soap opera had a story with Edwards' where the mother terminated the pregnancy.

I kept being hit by a single story – a story that emphasised there is no option but to terminate. It grieved me. My beautiful, affectionate and intelligent little girl, Hope, wouldn't be here if I had believed and acted on that.

Everything in me as a mother is focused on and programmed to protect my children: to protect them from physical harm, emotional hurt, damaging relationships, abuse, the list goes on. In the womb or out of the womb, they're my child and I want them to flourish.

Deciding whether to terminate for medical reasons can feel an incredibly difficult decision to make, and ending the pregnancy may be presented as the best option. We made our decision because we believe God has made each and every one of us, and it is up to Him to decide when our allocated time has come to an end. While, of course, support and not judgement should be offered no matter what people decide, it is worth noting families who let nature take its course rarely seem to feel regret, but only gratitude for the time they had.

Gratitude was our focus: I firmly felt any time we had with Hope alive would create incredibly treasured memories. I do not believe we have a right to health and ease and a long life. I know resilience and emotional strength are only built as we go through challenging times and hold on to our faith and believe that God is with us. It's not about who deserves what, as suffering is part of life. If Jesus suffered, then how can we assume we won't?

I now had the fire in my bones to tell Hope's story and present an alternative narrative with a distinctive ending. A friend offered a day in a local shepherd's hut, and it was absolutely beautiful. I napped, I read, I walked in nature, I sat in silence, and then I opened my laptop. The words flowed. As did fear. *I won't have enough words to fill a book. This won't be good enough. Am I wasting my time? What if no one reads it?*

The determination settled with this: if one person reads this and decides to continue a pregnancy, then it's worth it. It's one baby given a chance of life; one family deciding a baby's life, even if disabled or limited, is worth including in their number, in their story. It's saying yes to uncertainty and difficulty, but the other option is also one of grief and pain.

Yes, we have a wonderful happy ending to share. Praise God! I also know that Hope's life would be as cherished and awesome if she were in and out of hospital and never able to eat without a tube, or if she'd only lived a heartbreakingly short amount of time.

I returned to the shepherd's hut repeatedly, whenever a set of grandparents came to visit and could look after Hope. I knew it was a labour of love and would take a while, but now I had a vision to give me purpose and drive.

January 2024

As I sat in the shepherd's hut with my laptop and diaries, I reread old emails on my phone to make sure I was being as accurate as possible. When I was writing about the potential false positive prediction in the 'Late January' entry, I skim-read the email from Tracy from Be Not Afraid to see if I could understand it fully and explain it clearly.

Once I'd finished writing, a phrase nagged at me to include it, and I had to look over the email a number of times to find it. It was a detailed email and I found it in the middle of a long paragraph. The sentence that followed caught my breath, and I could not believe what I was reading. Tracy had written:

> Your ultrasound findings are not necessarily typical for babies with T18. It is also important to note that the NIPT results are actually looking at placental cells which we would expect to be like baby, but are not always. You could have a placenta with Trisomy and have a baby without Trisomy. That is very rare, but it could happen.

You could have a placenta with Trisomy and a baby without!

I could not believe it. Someone had told us it was possible! I have no memory of reading that sentence when I first read her email. One small sentence lost in the sea of a detailed email, skim-read and passed over as if it held no importance.

It was as if we'd struggled to navigate escaping a complex, twisting maze, only to find we'd had a map in our hands the whole time. And this map indicated there was a door to our left that took us straight outside. We could have potentially skipped ahead in our knowledge and understanding of what we were dealing with, had we taken this possibility on board. Although then the birth wouldn't have been such an incredible reveal!

I think writing the book has afforded me another chance to process it all, to dive deep into the experience and the emotions and then release it completely. It's allowing this story to become one of many, many chapters of our family history and not the defining one. I pray it is a story that brings hope and comfort to many and brings glory to God. As God gave life to Hope and has a plan and a purpose for her, so I trust this book into His hands for all He wants it to accomplish.

Acknowledgements

This book would not be in your hands if our 'village' didn't exist – all of the people who supported us throughout the time written about and since then.

First of all, I would like to thank the NHS staff mentioned here – none of you is named and all of you went above and beyond. We are grateful for all of your care and will always remember the myriad of ways you helped us. Special mention to the consultant who so kindly let us have extra time in scans to 'make memories', and to the wonderful nurses in SCBU. I do not take the NHS for granted!

Thank you to the local children's hospice who made special exemption for us and made the whole experience one of comfort and compassion. I have huge admiration for children's hospices and, while grateful we never ended up needing many of the offered services, benefited hugely from the preparation before the birth and the counselling afterwards.

Thank you to all the charities mentioned here: SOFT UK, Every Life Counts, Be Not Afraid, Zoe Faith and Remember My Baby. The peer support was incredible; to feel I was not alone and my range of emotions were understood and shared. Thank you to Vicky, Tracy, Dr Marty, Shaun, Kate and all the others at SOFT UK – who knew we'd be three years on and I'd be asking for permission to include your stories in a book? You're all excellent at what you do and change people's lives by being there at their time of need.

For all the families who graciously gave permission for their dear children's stories to be included, thank you. I hope you feel I did them justice and that they'll be remembered with love. For Hudson, Gabriel, Jovie, Hannah, Líadán, Kitty and all the other precious babies whose time on this earth was too short. Their legacy will live on.

Thank you to our church community who aided us immensely: meals, lifts, prayers, a listening ear, childcare, presents and cards. We felt so loved and so carried. Special mention to Matt and Paz, our pastors, and Alin and Dana who invested so much in us and in this book. You were the first to suggest it and showed generously how you believe in and support it. Thank you to all of our friends mentioned in the book: Peter and Andrea, James and Steph, Rowena and Charles, Georgina, Jo, Holly, Mallory, Rachel and Mariette and families, and to all those not mentioned by name but who were equally as wonderful to us! I apologise I can't name you all! Thank you to Lorraine for the first day in the shepherd's hut where the book was born. Thank you to all those on the Zoom call at the time of Hope's birth and the international community that had a day of prayer and fasting when we first received the diagnosis. You're incredible, and I am who I am today because of many of you.

Thank you to my first readers who were very gracious in their suggestions for improvement and comments on the manuscript! The book is better because of you: Jo C, Christina, Natasha and Kimmy.

Thank you to Instant Apostle for believing in this book enough to take it on and for coaching me through the publishing process. Thank you Nicki, Anne and Nigel, and abundant thanks to Sheila for editing with such accuracy and much patience with my many questions and comments.

Abundant gratitude to my parents, Keith and Janie, who looked after Hope so I could write this book. You've shaped me with values of resilience and perseverance which held me during this time and, of course, given me a solid foundation of faith in God and trust in His Word. You taught me to fly and have championed me every day of my life.

Lastly, thank you to Paul and the kids. You're my biggest blessings and greatest providers of joy. I am immensely grateful to be family with you and hope this book is a blessing to you. I love you with my whole heart and will never stop.

www.carryinghope.co.uk

carryinghopebook@gmail.com

carryinghopebook

carryinghopebook